Joint Forest Management in Assam

Joint Forest Management in Assam

M.M. Deka

2002
DAYA PUBLISHING HOUSE
DELHI-110035

ISBN 81-7035-266-5

Published by : **Daya Publishing House**
1123/74, Deva Ram Park
Tri Nagar, Delhi-110 035
Phone : 7103999
Fax : (011) 7199029
E-mail : dayabooks@vsnl.com
Website : www.dayabooks.com

Showroom : 4762-63/23, Ansari Road
New Delhi - 110 002
Ph.: 3245578, 3244987

Laser Composed by : **Vaishnav Graphics & Systems**
New Delhi - 110 055

Printed at : **Chawla Offset Printers**
Delhi-110052

PRINTED IN INDIA

Dedicated

To my father

Late Nabin Ch. Deka

PREFACE

Close association with the Joint Forest Management System in Assam as a petty worker in it from its very inception, I would feel the urge to analyse and understand how this great development programme was coming about, and what forces were contributing to it. In the course of my duties, I had much to do with explaining the nature, significance and the manifold aspects of J.F.M. to participants, villagers and non-officials which gave me some unique experience. That urge and this experience gave birth to the desire to write this book. In writing this book, my main purpose is to present a comprehensive picture of J.F.M. at Assam with special reference to Dhubri district. I have attempted to expound the ideology and objectives of J.F.M. as I have come to understand it. My understanding is that without knowing the theoretical aspects, the full conception of practical issues relating to J.F.M. programmes will be hardly possible. So, some theoretical ideas are presented in this book which can be practised in the field of J.F.M. activities of Assam. I do hope that the reader will also find some material of practical nature to think and to satisfy them; I have also gave attention on the actual problems that the J.F.M. workers of Assam are facing to implement in the field.

Dhubri district is something different from the others of Assam, as it touches Bangladesh and West Bengal. So, I am selecting Dhubri district as a special reference in J.F.M. system of Assam. Existence of ex-Zamindary forest of Assam (Brahmaputra valley) is found at the then Goalpara district at Dhubri is now a portion of Goalpara.

Experts are experts and for experts, this book may not be more. This book is meant for non-experts of J.F.M. and for the interested readers of North East as an outline sketch.

The most valuable contribution of this book makes J.F.M. as well as topics connected to it more approachable. Also, I have tried to give a consolidated picture of J.F.M. in policies and practice adopted by the various states of India. I can say without hesitation that at present this book provides authentic information on J.F.M. and its connecting lines. The various themes of this book were discussed with friends, family and a number of concerned and experienced people. As far as possible the book has tried to reflect the current development and trends of people's participation in forest within the country.

Writing a book requires a lot of time, concentration and knowledge etc. One's routine work gets disturbed. Over all, I am not a professional writer and the concept of people's participation at Assam is a quite a new one. An inexperienced writer, (I am) is drawing a new picture on a new concept. Presenting this book, the author's aim is to create a better awareness of the principles and practices of J.F.M. among practising persons including the participants. Positive criticism, errors and omissions will be highly acceptable to develop the book in future.

Last but, not the least, I am thankful to Mr. H.K. Sharma, A.F.S. (present Divisional Forest Officer, North Kamrup Forest Division and the present Principal of P.B. College, Gauripur, Mr. G.S. Pandey, Dr. Ajit Kr. Borua (Retd. Lect. of B.N. College) Dhubri, inspite of their various engagement of social and official circles, all went through the manuscript, and also M/S Charles Computer System, Dhubri and Sri Manik Roy, Gauripur for their labour in reflecting my poor hand writings into the computer monitor before sending the same to the press.

I expresses profound gratefulness to Mr. Anil Mittal of Daya Publishing House, New Delhi for his appreciation.

M.M. Deka
Gauripur, Dhubri (Assam)

CONTENTS

1
EX-ZAMINDARY FOREST OF DHUBRI DISTRICT

Dhubri is a thickly populated` district of Assam with a population density of about 470 per sq. km. The total geographical area of the district is 2838 sq. km. (Figures from 1991 census). The district bears about 31983 Hect. of Reserve Forest area covering 20 Nos. of R.F. and about 18420 Hect. of areas are under 10 Nos. of proposed Reserved Forests.

Prior to independence, all the forests under Dhubri Division were controlled by the local Zamindars. (Except the Guma R.F.) so, these forests are also known as Ex-Zamindary Forests. During their times, the Zamindars allowed some rights and concession to the local villagers which may be free or on payment of SAN-BAN Tax which include consumption of fire-wood, agriculture implements (Nagal) and house posts etc. Therefore, the local people preserved the forests as their own property, as their day to day requirement of forest produces came from the nearby forests. Further, the Zamindars maintained their forests, for economical benefits by exploiting the commercially valuable, matured and over matured trees. During those days, the main timber market was Dhaka (Now under Bangladesh). Timbers were marketed in log forms and transported by the river Brahmaputra and its tributaries such as Gangadhar, Godadhar, Tipkai, Sonkosh, Gaurang, etc. Forests were one of the major earning sources of Zamindars.

This system of management continued till 1951, when the Government enacted, "Assam State Acquisition of Zamindars Act. 1951" (Assam Act. xviii of 1951). Thus the zamindary system was abolished and these forests came under the control of State Government. The first "Working Scheme" for the forests was started by M.S. Islam, working plan officer in Oct./1962. Later on, L.C. Das took over the charge from him on 08-11-1962 who completed the field work during May 64 and prepared the first working scheme of Ex-Zamindary forests under Dhubri Division, which came under the orbit of Scientific Forest Management.

The Ex-Zamindary forest of Dhubri Division suffered a lot in past and is still in peril due to over exploitation during the zamindar administration to earn more and without following any scientific forest management. Principally, this caused irrepairable loss and damage of forests; second world war was also one of the reasons for damage of forests of the district; for example present Atharokota R.F. (966:80 Hect.), Bamunijhora R.F. (344:00 Hect.) and Rupshi R.F. of Dhubri Forest Division were under occupation of Army during this period. The ruins of buildings & roads found within the reserved forests bear the testimony of 2nd World War forests. The Rupshi Air Port which operated casually till 1997, was constructed by the British upon an established Tea Garden and the Tea Garden was raised by clearing the virgin forests as was done in other Tea Gardens of Assam in past.

After independence and the abolition of zamindary system of the then Goalpara district, the major problem of forests is the encroachment. In the first working scheme of forests, it was stated as follows:

"In recent years muslim population have increased to a large extent. They depend more on agriculture and on the neighbouring forests to live by unlike the local indigenous people". This practice is still continuing and increasing day by day, not only Muslims, but Santhals, Rajbanshis, Bodos, Ravas and Garos etc. are also causing destruction of forest crops and decreasing the forest areas. The other important problem is the indiscriminate felling of trees & smuggling of timbers etc. Many saw mills were installed within the Reserve Forests with valid licences. No Saw Millers of Assam can speak boldly that they have not done any single illegality in past. Many such illegalities were detected same as in the case of Saw Mills of Dhubri Division. One Plywood and Veneer mill & AMCO Match Factory, 18 Nos. of Saw Mills were working within this Division till the ban was imposed recently by the Hon'ble Supreme Court of India.

The illegalities in Dhubri Division started since the time of abolition of zamindary system. As no forests were declared as Reserve Forests on the same day, rather it took a long period to cross the hurdle of sec. 4 to sec. 26 of the Assam Forest Regulation, 1891. For instance, Mahamaya and Monglajhora, the two biggest forests of Dhubri Division were declared as R.F. on 10.7.61 vide Government Notification No : For/Sett/372/61/30 and For/Sett/374/61/30 respectively after 10 years. Till today, many of the proposals are in the process for declaration of Reserve Forest such as paglijhora, parbotjoar etc. This was mentioned by L.C. Das in his first working scheme of this Division which was prepared for 5 years commencing on 1st of Oct. 1964 as follows : "This is a sad state of affairs that the proposals are lying for such a long period giving full scope for disappearance of forest high potential in the area (sal forests) by illegal felling during this transitory period". Even the zamindars approached the judiciary and overstepped into the floor of Supreme Court of India where they obtained the injunction order against acquisition.

The forests under Dhubri Division predominately of sal forest types and the use of sal timbers (multifarious) starting from fire-wood to Railway sleepers, illegal collection of fire-wood from the forests is the menace for the Forest Department as well as to the forest covers. The high rate of consumption of Fire-wood can be estimated easily from the figures that out of the total population of the district of 13,32000 only, 7340 families are using L.P.G. for cooking purposes. The percentage of kerosene oil, use is almost negligible. The people of Dhubri District mainly depend upon forest for fire-wood.

For this purpose, not only the matured trees are felled but also most of the young plantations and regeneration of sal is badly damaged resulting not only in economical losses but also in damaging the fragile ecosystem of this district. About 14549 hects. of plantations were raised within the forests of Dhubri Division since 1951. But the future of these plantations are quite gloomy. It is estimated that 0.28 cubic meter of fuel wood per capita, equivalent to about 0:2 tonnes fuel wood is necessary. But in practice, officially the supply of fuel wood at present is zero and from this, the problems of fuel wood consumption can be easily imagined.

From the above discussion we come to the inference that the forests of Dhubri Division are badly in the grip of land hangering organisations and smugglers of timber and firewood. In fact, this is the actual picture everywhere in Assam. If it is allowed to continue, within a short time, all the forests will vanish with its valuable flora & fauna and we shall be answerable to our next generations. The rate of destruction of forests in Assam is high but it is higher in Dhubri District. But for our survival, we have to save the forests.

After various alternatives made to protect the Forest eco-systems of the country of Joint forest management were evolved in India, 24 states have already adopted the joint forest management out of which West Bengal is the pioneer State with 2423 forest committees which protect 390919 hect. covering 33 per cent of its forests area. In Andhra Pradesh, beneficiaries are allowed to consume 100 per cent of non-timber forest produce and 50 per cent of timber. Tripura is the only state of North-East India who accepted the JFM system for the first time.

Forest protection and regeneration committees are to be formed for the protection of forests and the beneficiaries (members of the committee) will get the surplus out of the harvest from silviculture thinnings and main fellings. After meeting the domestic needs, the left out will be sold by the forest department, to 50 per cent of the net receipt from silvicultural thinnings and 25 per cent from main fellings. Also the receipt from the harvest of social forestry plantations will be distributed among the beneficiaries after deduction of cost of plantation. Bodo Autonomous council also decided to implement JFM as notified vide memo No. BAC/FPM. 10/96-97/77 dated Kokrajhar the 17th Feb, 97. Here the beneficiaries assured the Government that the beneficiaries will be on the basis of 80:20. Almost all the forest areas of Dhubri Division now within the jurisdiction of BAC, without going to the details of the proposal, it can be predicted that JFM will surely help in protection of forests specially at Dhubri Division. It will be a symbiotic relationship between the forests and neighbouring people.

During the last May 1998, (on 07-05-98) at village Modati within Monglajhora R.F. raised 20 Hect. of plantations in four equal different plots by the local villagers. The villagers of Modati created four Forest protection committees constituting 20-50 members in each committee having one President and one Secretary.

They are

1.	Sri Udash Rava	-	President
	Sri Dhanpati Rava	-	Secretary
2.	Sri Narayan Ch. Rava	-	President
	Sri Nehar Ch. Rava	-	Secretary
3.	Sri Chaiman Rava	-	President
	Sri Joty Jiban Rava	-	Secretary

4. Sri Kisan Kr. Rava - President
   Sri Dhanindra Rava - Secretary

The idea of people's participation in the protection of forests under Dhubri Division germinated during 1983-84 in the mind of Sri K.N. Dev Goswami I.F.S. the then D.F.O. of Dhubri Division and now the chief conservator of forests, Social Forestry, Assam. He mobilised the local people with the help of the members of Parbotjoar Janajati Kath Bebasaye Sangha along with the writer, who was the then Range Officer, Rupshi Range. On 25.01.84, the first Forest Protection Committee was constituted at Rupshi Range under Dhubri Forest Divn. Perhaps it was the first Forest Protection Committee of Assam constituted by local people, with the aim to protect and preserve the forests involving the local people. The said committee was headed by Sri Bhim Chandra Brahma, Bashbari. Later on, after a gap of about 7 (seven) years on 01.05.91 Paraura Sesargaon Tilapara Forest Protection Committee was constituted under the presidentship of late Hitendra Dev Nath where in Sri Chitra Dhar Ray of village Sesargaon was the Secretary. Again on 08-05-95 the villagers of Sesergaon, Nathpara, Malgari, Kauragaon, Vouspara and Saktola all under Dhubri Forest Division another Forest Protection Committee was constituted with Sri Santosh Kr. Sarma as President and Sri Nripen Ch. Nath as the Secretary. Likewise, now more or less 20 (twenty) Forest Protection Committees were formed upto May 1998 within Dhubri Forest Divn. and the performances of these committees are fully satisfactory. Hence, it is crystal clear that some of the local people are really interested from the core of their heart to protect the forests.

It is therefore, revealed that forests of Dhubri Forest Division could be managed easily by involving the local people, like some other States of the country. Sooner or later, the practice of joint Forest Management is the best way to manage and sustain the forests of this division in a scientific and perpetual manner.

2

History of Participatory Forest Management at Dhubri District

"Creation of a massive people's movement with the involvement of man for achieving the objectives and to minimise pressure on existing forest" is one of the objects of Indian National Forest Policy, 1988. Prior to this policy, the idea was practised in Purulia District of West Bengal in 1970 at Karandi village with the formation of "Gramer Khas Jami Jangal Abong Krishi Abad Sangrakshan Committee." Initially, this committee controlled 60 Hect, of sal forest. It is the first protection committee in India with the participation of local people. Now, the participatory forest management is accepted by Government of India.

Similarly in Dhubri Forest Division on 25th January, 1984 a meeting of the Executive committee of "Parbatjowar Janajati Kath Bebasaye Sangha" Bashbari was held, which was presided by Sri Bhim Ch. Braha. A total of 70 (seventy) members were present in this meeting and in the first resolution of the meeting, it was decided to constitute a forest protection committee for the development and protection of forest under Rupshi Range of Dhubri Forest Division. Again on 20th June, 1984, a meeting of the Executive committee was held under the presidentship of Sri Bhim Ch. Brahma where 64 (sixty four) members were present and it was decided in the Resolution No.5 to constitute areawise (villagewise) Forest Protection Committees to control the illegal felling of trees and timber smuggling. The Forest protection committee under the banner of Parbatjowar Janajati Kath Bebasayee Sangha, Bashbari performed their duties and responsibilities with hundred per cent success from 25th January, 1984 to 15th December, 1984. During this period, illegal felling of trees within Rupshi Range jurisdiction was reduced to a large extent. Smuggling of timber was almost zero. Large number of buffalo, carts etc, were seized, besides a number of accused were arrested and handed over to police or forwarded to the Chief Judicial Magistrate, Dhubri for judicial trial with the help of an active co-operation of the members of this forest protection committee. Those were the golden days for Rupshi Range of Dhubri Forest division in the line of forest protection through the people's participation.

Prior to 1983-84, the condition of the field staff of forest department starting from Forest Guard to D.F.O. in the protection of forests were just like that of asking a lamb to control a pack of wolves in the Dhubri division. Under these circumstances the present chief conservator of Forest Social Forestry, Assam Mr. K.N. Dev. Goswami I.F.S. joined as D.F.O. on 18-9-83 at Dhubri Forest Division. He (18-9-83 to 11-9-84) had evolved an idea to involve the local people, specially the Tribal people of Dhubri Forest Division for the protection of forest. The writer had an opportunity to serve as a Forest Range officer, Rupshi Forest Range during this period. Now, after an interval of more than one and a half decade, the memories still knock, how the then D.F.O. Sri Dev Goswami passed his sleepless nights at Tribal villages to motivate the local people in protection of forest under Dhubri Forest Division. As a result, his ideas took shape as a reality and with his valuable guidance and suggestions, the first Forest Protection Committee of Assam was formed at Dhubri District.

But these golden days came to an end and his noble courageous venture and labour went in vain, after he handed over the charge of Dhubri Forest Division on 21-9-1984. A meeting of the Parbatjowar Janajati Kath Babsayee Sangha, Bashbri was held on 15th December 1984 in which Sri Bhim Ch. Brahma was the President and a total of 56 (Fifty six) members were present in this meeting. In the resolution No. 5 of this meeting, it was decided that if the government issued permit from the timber stock of Rupshi Range then all the help and co-operation for the protection of forests shall be withdrawn. But, no body came forward to listen the cry and honest demand of the Forest Protection Committee. Even in the resolution No. 8 of this meeting, it was decided that 5 (five) representative members will go to Dispur to explain the grievances that no timber permit should be issued from the timber stock of Rupshi Range. The representatives acted accordingly but the results were without any fruits. Permits, were issued to the outside timber contractors from the timber depot of Rupshi thus depriving the local people and for this reason, all the members of the Forest Protection Committee ceased to extend their co-operation. The results are now best known to all. Random illegal felling of trees started again. The Forest Protection Committee also became defunct.

Good ideas and thoughts never die. Hence, after the gap of about 7 (seven) years, the same idea and thoughts of Sri K.N. Dev Goswami, I.F.S. germinated on 1st May/ 1991 at Dhubri Forest Division. A new Forest Protection Committee was constituted at Parura-Sesargaon-Tilapara in which late Hitendra Dev Nath was selected as President and Sri Chitrdhar Roy was the General Secratary of the Committee. The said meeting was presided over by Sri Parimal Ch. Roy F.R. the then Forest Range Officer, Salkocha Forest Range. The performance of this Forest Protection Committee is still found to be satisfactory. But, they had some grievances which were reflected in the report of the Secretary dated 4th April/1993. One of the grievances of the committee was that no senior forest official rendered co-operation to them. One of the notable event of the Parura-Tilapara Forest Protection Committee was that on 6th Oct/91, the Jury which comprised 5 (five) members and was selected by the committee sentenced coporal punishment to one Sri Sutku Roy who had stolen barbed wire from the Tilapara social forestry plantations, by caning 5 (five) times publicly. This was decided in the meeting which was presided over by late Hiteswar Dev Nath on 6th Oct/1991.

Again after the gap of about of 5 (Five) years on 6th May/1996, the villagers of Sesargaon, Matpara, Belguri, Kouragaon, Vouspara and Saktola under Dhubri Forest Division, another Forest Protection Committee was constituted wherein Sri Santosh Kr. Sharma was selected as president and Sri Nripen Ch. Nath as the secretary. The said committee imposed social punishment to Sri Faguna Boro, Sri Karthing Boro and Sri Padmalachan Boro, who illegally felled trees inside forest. As desired by the Gaonboura (village head man) the punishment was awarded to all the three accused persons to bow down and touch feet of all the public present in the meeting openly. This was decided on 26th Oct/1996.

It is reliably learnt that more than 60 (sixty) Forest Protection Committees were formed during 1997-98 having more than 1000 members, within Dhubri Forest Division, also, there is chance to constitute more Forest Protection Committees, with the aim to protect, develop and extend the forest of this district. From these historical facts, one can easily come to the inference that the prospect of Forest Protection Committees of Dhubri District is bright and this is the only tool to protect, develop and extend the Forests under Dhubri Forest Division.

It is worth while to mention that for the benefits of the members of Forest protection Committees and to help and assist the growers and traders of forest crops in

Assam, the Assam Agriculture Produce Market Act 1972 (Assam Act, XXIII 1974) has come forward, to which President of India assented on 3rd Sept/74. In this act "Agriculture produce" is defined as follows:

Agricultural produce means and includes any produce whether processed or non-processed of agriculture, horticulture, animal husbandry, pisciculture, sericulture and forest as specified in the schedule. As mentioned in schedule (1) lac (2) Gum and (3) the timber is treated as forest products.

Hence, for the agriculturist, specially the forest dwellers and neighbouring forests, the legal value of paddy and rice is equivalent to forest product as per the provision of this Act. But this legal value is to be equalised to the social and economical values which is possible through the people's participation, specially at Dhubri District. The existing Forest Protection Committees of Dhubri District tells us that they are not alone rather the State Agriculture Marketing Board, Assam is also with them besides the Assam Forest Department.

3

Joint Forest Management in North East India

The system of management of Forest with active co-operation of local people is commonly known as Joint Forest Management (J.F.M.) system. The very idea of this system is to manage the forest "with the people". As in the past the system "For the People" is now found to be totally frustrating. In Assam working plans of different forests miserable failed to fulfil their objects, specially in sustainable supply of Forest Produce. India has 15 per cent of the world human population and 16 per cent of cattle population but having less than one per cent of the total productive forest area of the world. Also, more than 67 per cent of Indian people live in villages. India is the seventh largest country in the world with the area of 3287593 Sq. km. and the second largest populated country in the world with population of about 84.5 million (1991 census). It stretches 3220 km. from North to South and 2980 km. from East to West. So, how difficult the problem of management, conservation and expansion of forests is, it can be easily imagined. Aiming to solve the problem, the idea of J.F.M. was evolved within the soil of India. This new system will change the past system of forest management. Also, it will cause radical change to human attitude as J.F.M. will replace century old centralised Forest Management System. In the past, and even today, in the name of scientific forest management, the Indian forests have contributed only to the timber contractors and owners of the wood based heavy industries etc. but nothing for the forest dweller, the poor Indian people. Based on experience, the Ministry of Environment and Forest issued a circular on 1st June/1990 (No. 621/89-P.P.) to involve the villagers in management and protection of forests. Giving full support to this circular uptill now, 20 states adopted resolutions to implement JFM. They are Andhra Pradesh, Arunachal Pradesh, Bihar, Gujarat, Haryana, Himachal Pradesh, Jammu & Kashmir, Karnataka, Kerala, Madhya Pradesh, Maharashtra, Nagaland, Orissa, Punjab, Rajasthan, Tamil Nadu, Tripura, Uttar Pradesh, West Bengal and Assam. Presently, 12000 Forest Protection Committees are formed throughout the country and they are managing 1.5 million hectares of forests. Some of the salient features of J.F.M. system of North East States of India are described below with relation to other states.

Development of J.F.M. at Nagaland is highly encouraging. The state is having 16579 Sq. km. of area and population of 1209546. (1991 census) The main peculiarity of Nagaland is its land holding pattern and virtually any forestry development could not be achieved without the prior consent and active cooperation of the land owners. In fact, Nagaland having 85.3 per cent of forest area is owned by villagers which Forest Department having no direct control over it. After considering all aspects, the Government of Nagaland accepted J.F.M. system vide Notification No. FOR. 153/80 (Vol-II) Kohima dated 5th March/1997. In this scheme, the Government shall bear the financial burden along with technical assistance with the active participation of the land owners or land owning communities. Remarkable object of J.F.M. at Nagaland is to create a wood-based economy for the people, besides other common ideas. Members of the committee have to pay Rs. 20.00 (Twenty) annually which is not found in other J.F.M. committees of India except in

Nagaland. The site selection for implementation of JFM at Nagaland is done carefully as they have decided that the area should be at least 30 Hect. in a compact and preferably on the sides of National High Way, State High Ways, village roads even to any sites having trackable roads. As the Forest Department is the funding agency, hence for the Non-Government lands, the royalty shall be realised from the harvest crops at the current rate and on Government lands, 20 per cent of it is earned by participants and 80 per cent goes to the state exchequer. Tenure of the committee is five years but no where in India such a long term is fixed for Forest Protection Committees constituted under J.F.M.

In Arunachal Pradesh J.F.M. comes out as per the Notification No. FOR 104/D-4/90/Vol-I dated Itanagar the 3rd October/1997. Area of this state is 83,743 Sq. km. having population of 8,64,558 (1991 census). The important feature of composition of the Forest Protection Committees of the State is; involvement of woman participants. As not less than 30 per cent of the total registered members shall have to be women, the Village, Forest Management Committee (V.F.M.C.) must be registered under Society's Registration Act. The members of the Executive Committee of V.F.M.C. shall have power to seize illegal timber and other forest produce and have the power to levy fines for unauthorised or illegal activities on any of the member of the V.F.M.C. Benefits will be shared as fifty per cent on Government account, 25 per cent equally to the beneficiaries and balance 25 per cent to the Village Development Fund. Direct financial implication on the part of Forest Department for implementing this scheme. Women constitute about fifty per cent of the total population of India and is therefore one half of the total work force available to the nation. "The women of India have been and will always remain equal partners in the progress of the nation" said

Indira Gandhi which is reflected practically now in the J.F.M. Programme of Arunachal Pradesh.

Tripura has geographical area of 10,488 Sq. km. having population of 2,757,205. The J.F.M. programme came out by the Government Resolution No. F17 (1401/4) For-Dev/90-91/470-30-529 dt. 20-12-1991. In this state, Forest Protection and Regeneration Committees (F.P.R.C.) are formed usually limited to 5 Hect. per beneficiary for natural regeneration and 2 Hect. for intensive planting. A unit, usually with 500 Hect. for natural regeneration and 300 Hect. for artificial regeneration so as to ensure effective protection and management is prescribed for implementing the scheme. The F.P.R.C. will get 50 per cent of the total harvest including silvicultural thinning and main felling for satisfying the bonafide domestic needs of the beneficiaries.

Tripura is a state where more than 70 per cent of the area is full of hills and undulating high lands. About 60 per cent of the geographical area is under forest out of which 39 per cent is Reserve Forest. As the state is having less than 40 per cent of area outside the forest hence the rehabilitation of tribal people outside the forest is the basic problem for the Government. However, under this crucial circumstances, the J.F.M. grows up and the history of this programme at Tripura is very interesting. Sri Subod Ranjan Sur a commerce graduate hailling from Rudijala, Melaghar started Farm Forestry with the advice of the local Forest Range Officer in early eighties. They organised Acharya J.C. Bose Briksha Mitra Sangha during November/1987 with 10-12 youths including man and women, promoting farm forestry with the guidance of Forest Department. Forest Department of Tripura suspended the programme of Farm Forestry since 1990-91 as the scheme had been transferred to Rural Development Department. But the Forest Department took the youth group for their past experience, their ready acceptability to the villagers and their association with the Nehru Yuba Kendra for implementation of the project of participatory Forest Management. Another group of tribal youths (Aitorma) in the adjacent village of Mohanbhog motivated the people to raise horticulture and sericulture garden nearby in the non-forest waste land area. The then Director of Industries R.K. Singh supplied the mulberry cuttings free of cost and a small project under Decentralised People's Nursery under a 'buy back' arrangement was awarded to Aitorma. They raised Gamari seedlings in the nurseries and earned Rs. 12,000 at the end of the season after supplying the required quantities of seedlings to the department. Supply of mulberry cuttings to the Sericulture Department continued and was extended to the local people. In this way, the concerned forest personnel after proper orientation and motivation extended support to 230 beneficiary families creating consciousness and awareness for conservation of forests in their own interest both in short and long run since 1991. Fortunately Tripura is the 8th state in the country and it stands first in North East to bring out an enabling resolution for participatory Forest Management in the name of J.F.M.

The development of J.F.M. mainly deals with the forest personnel. They should think that they are the social workers. The work-style of Forest personnel should not be like police transparency to the public is necessary to develop J.F.M. Once Forest Officers start believing the people and are mentally prepared to help the poor, half of the battle is won. They should keep in mind that the forest personnel are the developers of the society and they have to think for the development of the society. It is not the fact that the villagers are unqualified, they may not have obtained the qualification certificates from colleges or universities but the qualification obtained from long experience is much more valuable than the certificates of colleges or universities. So, their qualification in practical field should always be honoured specially in tree cultivation.. J.F.M. workers of forest personnel compromise the ideas and thoughts with those of the villagers. Exchange of ideas and thought always produces a solid finding and this is to be implemented in the field of J.F.M. to achieve success of the programme.

V.K. Bahuguna rightly says –"The conversion of a hostile population living in the fringes of forest areas into friends and ultimately into resource managers and resource users is the fundamental underlying objective of the J.F.M. approach." Villagers should get the chance to be resource manager and resource users within their jurisdiction which they are capable to mange and use. This environment is to be created by the forest personnel in J.F.M. Grass root level political workers should be trained and motivated to act jointly for improving the foundation of the life supporting resources like trees within society. As in India, even in our state also, political leaders specially the grass root political workers are more close to the villagers than any other society developers of government agencies. Government officers are always professional administrators in India. Hence still there are good number of sceptical forest officers at senior level, not to talk of lots of junior field forest staff (In Assam) who are not very clear about this new system of forest management (JFM). But it is crystal clear to all that forest extension, conservation programme etc. can not be successful without the willing support and co-operation of the people.

In Assam, encroachment and illegal felling are the twin problems in management of forests. Presently our 260087. 16 Hect. of Reserve Forest areas is in the grip of encroachers. On the other hand, we have only 21 per cent forest areas. So, it is almost necessary to increase another 12 per cent of forest areas within a short time which is only possible by JFM raising forest crops outside the forest areas. The same encroachment problem is smoothly solved in Andhra Pradesh by introducing JFM among the encroachers. It is remarkable that about 5000 hectare of encroachments in Reserve Forest made by non-locals have been evicted by local tribals who have formed village Vana Sumarakshene Sumithi (VSS) at Andhra Pradesh. Another achievement of JFM at Aravalli Afforestation Project in Haryana has planted 17,000 Hect. of village common lands without fencing by involving the local people. But in our state, fencing is one of the major expensive item in plantation. One of the unique duties and responsibilities of VVS at Andhra Pradesh is to apprehend the forest offenders and hand them over to the authorities concerned to take action and all such cases where forest offenders have been handed over to the concerned forest officials, the concerned forest authority will be responsible to report back the action taken by them to the Managing Committee. In case, where the Members of the Managing Committee feel that the punishment inflicted does not commensurate with the gravity of the offence, the member secretary of the Managing Committee shall report the matter to D.F.O. for futher action.

The details of J.F.M. Notification of Assam is mentioned separately in this book.

4
Forest is For People

The two words "Ecology" and "Environment" are related with Forest but these two "Es" are meaningless for the villagers of Assam living within and around the forests. For them the word "Economy" is most meaningful. So to get the support from people in foresty operations, economic benefits are to be shared with local people. Other high sounding words does not give anything to the forest dwellers or local people and even to the forest.

After the treaty of YANDABO, 1826 A.D. the East India Company (The British Government) assumed the Governance of Assam. Forest Department of India came in existence since 1864 with D. Brandis as the first Inspector General of Forests. Assam Forest Regulation. 1891 (Regulation 7 of 1891) came after 65 year of British occupation. Hence, these rules and regulations were created only in the interest of the British crown. For instance, Assam Forest Regulation and Indian Forest Act. does not think anything for the forest dwellers, local tribal people. This was reflected on the report of Scheduled Tribes Commission in 1961. Presented by the veteran freedom fighter U.N. Dhabar. This commission observed that the full control of tribal communities over forest resources was changed into merely some rights by the 1894 forest policy. Even these rights were reluctantly accepted merely as concessions by 1952 policies which did not mean much in concrete terms. Recognition of rights of forest dwellers in the management of forest was necessary to develop the forest and to change the forest policy accordingly was the idea of this commission. It is an established fact that in past the capitalist enterprises were encouraged in protection of forests even at Assam for their own interest without considering others interests. Not to speak of other, the use of barbed wire fencing in different plantations of Assam Forest Department is one of the example as not a single centimeter of barbed wire is produce within the state. As a result, almost the whole amount spent for fencing materials goes directly out side the state. This can be easily replaced by the local old traditional fencing system with the help of indigenous materials. Steps are taken by social forestry sector of Assam introducing life hedge fencing with local suitable tree species without using any barbed wire.

On the other hand, inference of acid test statement of B.K. Ray Barman, Council for Social Development, New Delhi is very significant–

'The field level forest officials are a colonial creation' which is basically correct. Even their functions are also colonial in nature. Observation of Forest Policy 1894 was ...."The inferior subordinates of the Forest Department are perhaps as reliable as can be expected on the pay we can afford to give, but their morality is no higher than that of the uneducated classes from which they are drawn". From this veiw, the tendency of the rulers to the local person can easily be calculated and on the other side the petty forest officials were made scapegoats. The successors of the colonial rulers were also found on the same path.

For instance, Imperial Forest Service of British kingdom was abundant in independent India. But again after 18 years of Independence Indian Forest Service was created since 1st July 1966. In this case S.P. Aiyar rightly says – It is curious.

Services which had been abolished because they were considered to be the creations of an imperial power and running contrary to the genuine spirit of provincial autonomy were again sought to be resurrected. (Constitutional History Indian – A.C.Kapar.).

History is necessary for future guidance. From the experience of the past history, the new Indian National Forest Policy was framed out in 1988 in which massive people's movement was incorporated in protection of forests. Committee on 'Forest and Tribals' set up by the Government of India, in their report submitted in 1982 suggested that climated of participation needs to be created among the tribals who revolt against the encroachment and destruction of forests. The slogan "Forest is for the poeple" is to be implemented in practice and for this bureaucratic arrogance and capitalist style should be avoided. As stated by Dr. B.D. Sharma, Ex-Vice Chancellor, North East Hill University, Shillong, "Forest should be started with the wood cutter" is to be tried inside the forest of Assam. He described an experience of his own at "Planning in Forest in Tribal Areas" as follows :

In Jhabua, M.P. all passenger trains reaching Dahod in the evening are full of Bhils with headloads of firewood. No forester can afford to challenge the Bhil because he is prepared to die for it, as this is the only substance for him. An experiment was tried at Kerala by forming co-operactive societies among these people. Initially Forest Department was opposed to the idea of forming co-operative societies among these people. But later on agreed on this idea as this hungry man could not be prevented from entering the forest so long as he has no other alternatives. On this co-operative society was formed these poor men became the protectors of the forest and they did not allow other unauthorised persons to enter the forest. The members of the co-operative society are allowed to collect the dry firewood and deliver their headload at the co-operative depots to get the fixed fair price. Later on, fast growing species plantations were started inside the forest areas with these members. At last, the predator of forests become active partner in the fuelwood plantation programmes. Similar problem is being faced by the forest of Dhubri District. Dhubri passenger train is loaded with illegal fire-wood. Every evening thousands of men and women are coming out from the forest with headload of fire-woods. Forest personnel have tried their level best to control these illegalities within their orbits of powers and capacities. But results are not encouraging. Hence, a new policy is necessary for the benefits of both the forest and the wood cutters.

Cupidity could not be controlled. We have to mention the name of Mr. Saneswar Bora, Ex. Agriculture Minister, Assam during 1978, who introduced the tea plantations among the youth of Upper Assam individually. Presently, well known to all as Mini Tea garden is the results of thoughts and ideas of Sri Soneswar Bora. as prior to 1978, no one took any steps for this venture. Tea plantations were confined only within Tea gardens by the rich tea planters. Now this experiment of Mr. Soneswar Bora proves to be very fertile and thosands of educated young youth are engaged in these plantation giving relief to the Government from the unemployment problems. Similar attempts can be tested in the light of the suggestions of National Commission on Agriculture 1976 by providing employment opportunities to the forest dwellers. But it was found just opposite in respect of employment in forestry sector. In a paper, contributed to a seminar held at Tata Institute of Social Science in 1979, it was stated that in 1950-51 about 4 lakh persons were engaged in forestry and in 1971, the corresponding figure came down to approximately 2.5 Lakhs. Same conditions are prevailing in our state also. Employment potential in forestry section of Assam is decreasing day by day. Employment opportunities are only possible by total land use and rational utilization of land through scientific forestry management. Tree farming for food, fodder, timber and village industries raw materials will give an assured and independent employment to the forest people. Establishing some heavy wood base industries never satisfy the needs of forest dwellers or nearby people of forests. Commercial plantation is to be raised by the authority in regard to heavy wood based industries by their own resources. In Assam more than 40 big plywood mills were established and we were proud to produce more than 60% of total production of plywood and 60% of tea chests in the country. But this pride has now proved to be futile and the proudness has now failed to maintain the sustenance. The situation reached such a state that the Appex of Indian Judiciary. The Supreme Court had to come forward to prevent the felling of trees within Assam and other North East states.

The definition of forests is also contradictory and now the definition of forest presented by Sunderlal Bahuguna as written in "Forests and Tribals – The chipko approach" is found to be very comprehensive in comparison to the other three established old definitions of forest. According to him, "A forest is a community or a society of living beings, of which tree is the biggest. In this society trees, herbs, shrubs, grasses, insects, birds and other animals are all the members and dependent to each other. Human beings are also one of the members of this society". But with the expansion of human civilization and human development, the forests have continuously disappeared. Now the question is that the human development is necessary but the existence and development of forest cannot be ignored. We can not allow to continue the destruction of forests at the rate of 32 hectares per minute as going on now in the tropical rain forests.

By pushing the different problems backwards and experience gathered from the past, the participatory forest management system is the only suitable and attractive means specially for Ex-zamindary forest of Dhubri District along with other forests of Assam, the past centralised management system has now totally failed. Common people got nothing from this. Protection of forest with arms and weapons is also not very much effective. This feudal attitude will not save our forests, rather it is a mockery of democracy. Hence, forest is for people is the best solution, specially for Assam. Presently more than 20 states of India have adopted this practice of participatory forest management in the name of Joint Forest Management system (up to 1998) and they are saying to us that if we can do so can you? Surely, we can do it and the colonial looks of Assam Forests are bound to end here with the formation of participatory Forest Management System by the democratic ways.

5

JOINT FOREST MANAGEMENT IS THE BLESSING FOR ASSAM

Joint Forest Management (J.F.M.) has the symbiotic relationship between forest department and local people living by the surrounding or inside forest. National Forest Policy 1988, creates a new era in the management of forest where rights of the people living and around the forests are recognized. Also, it facilitates the local people to be the partner of forest department, in creation, protection and development of forests. The news item published in "The Asomiya Pratidin" dated 29th January, 1999 says that the Hon'ble Forest Minister of Assam, Late Nagen Sarma stated that the JFM has started on experimental basis at Dhubri, Kamrup and Goalpara districts. No doubt, it is appreciable to all, specially the poor villagers who depend mainly upon forests. The State having geographical area of 78,438 sq. km. with population of 2241322 (1991 census), it is very distressing that we are suffering from twelve per cent shortage of forest area. In this position. J.F.M. is the only means to extend the forest areas besides the protection of existing forests. Major sources of the extension of forest are the road side fallow lands. Assam is having the following National High Ways:

1. 31 - (a) Boxirhat to Guwahati

   (b) North Salmara to Jogighopa

   (c) Bijni to Srirampur

2. 37 - Panchartna to Chaikhowa
3. 36 - Nagoan to Dimapur
4. 38 - Tinsukia to Lekhapari
5. 39 - Numiligarah to Dimapur
6. 40 - Guwahati to Dauki
7. 51 - Krishnai to Tura
8. 52 - Baihata to Tezpur
9. 50 - Badarpur to Silchar
10. 58 - Tinsukia to Tezu

Total length of these National Highways within Assam,is 2296 km. which is apparently too less as compared to other parts of the country. In North East India there is only 28.88 Sq. km. of areas are covered while 48.79 km. are available in per 100 sq. km of areas in other states. However, scope is there to raise 2296 km. road side strip plantation which will give us another 2296 hect. plantations which is more or less equivalent to eight reserve forest under Dhubri Division.

(Rupsi 123.30 Hect. Athorokotha 996.00 Hect. Bamunijhora 344.0 Hect. Lalkura 154.40 Hect. Tipkai 116.00 Hect. Silkikhata 172.00 Hect Tilapara 116.00 Hect=Total 2259.70 Hect.) This is the picture of only National Highways besided we have state highways-2106 km. state PWD roads-30086 km. and railway lines-2467 km. Whose available area of tree cultivation is much more than that of the reserve forest areas in Dhubri division. Social forestry sector of Assam Forest Department successfully implemented this scheme and road side plantations in many places found imense success. But the progress of this scheme is very slow due to the non-availbility of funds. Also, no social organisations nor any NGOs are coming out voluntarily to plant trees on the road sides. If the time passes like wise, the road side land will also be encroached by the land hungry people and another problem will arise to vacate those lands to raise plantation. So, by introducing JFM, this problem can be solved easily by giving proper share of forest products to the members of the committee. Similar attempts are to be taken on the sides of the embankments of the rivers of Assam, irrigation channels etc. For this, JFM workers of the forest department have to evolve the plan and to find out the ways and means to execute this on the field. Government has initiated a scheme for 100 days employment annually to the villagers, who live under proverty line through Employment Assurance Scheme during IX plan period commencing from 1st April/1997. With the help of this scheme, there is ample scope to cover the road side areas by tree plantation within short span of time. For this, we require correct information, perfect imagination and planning. Nagas are very fond of meat; they consume more meat as food. So, the prospect of leather industries are more bright in Nagaland. But this plan is purely based on theoretical ideas. In practice, Nagas eat meat with the skins, Hence, though meat consumption is more but the skins are not available at all to run the leather industries. Micro plan is most essential element for JFM. For instance, if we have to plan for supply of the leaf fodder to the cattles or the surrounding villagers then we have to consider that for one pair of cow (one is dry and the other having milk) who lives solely on stall feeding of leaves then we have to plant 1500 trees and for this purpose only, one third km. of strip plantation is required. In Assam kathal (*Artocarpus integrifolia*) is one of the important timer species. Its fruit is also used as fodder and leaves are suitable food for stall feeding to cattle.

In JFM, integrated planning related to the villagers such as Dairy, Horticulture, Fruit processing and preservation etc. are necessary. Fruit bearing local timber species such as kathal, Am (*Mangifera indica*), Jam (*Eugenia jambolana*) etc will surely serve the various demands of the villagers including the economical benefits instead of planting hundred per cent commercial trees. It has been experienced by the forest personnel throughout the country that some tribal people use teak timbers as fire-wood and they damage the teak plantation as it is not necessary for them. Similar instance is found at Mussaljhora RRF (*Alokjhora*) under Dhubri Forest Division where teak plantations of whole of the PRF (134.30 hects) was completely consumed in long past as fire-wood by the surrounding villagers. Now it is under consideration of the forest department to regenerate the area with viable teak root stocks. On micro planning in JFM, these points have to be seriously considered as social dimension of the JFM programme is much more interesting than the development of forest. In JFM programme, forest department should help the village development in all aspects like education, health and even the small savings etc. To make the JFM successful at Assam transparency in all transactions and sharing of benefits must be maintained. In this case procedure of Andhra Pradesh is found very successful and suitable for Assam. There, the whole monetary transaction is being done in an absolutely transparent manner. Firstly a copy of the estimated expenditure on various works to be done as planned jointly in the microplane, is given to the committee. The amount required for the work is kept in the Bank under a joint account with the President of the committee and the Forester who acts as a Secretary. The amount is drawn through joint signature. Importing labour from outside the area or plantation centres and engaging labours without giving importance to the committees is always against the principle of JFM. Again, in Andhra Pradesh, the new JFM inititive commenced with the inauguration of Chintalpudo Vana Samarak Shana Samithi (VSS) in West Godavary district by the Hon'ble Chief Minister of the state on 11th

Feb./1996. Simultaneously, all the legislators inaugurated VSS in the respective constituencies. These acts encourage the village poeple and the grass root political workers. Initially they were badly criticised by the newspaper of the state but later on all the Andhra people understood the actual facts and benefit, and now support comes to JFM programme from all angles.

It is commonly said by the Foresters that low investment in forestry sector has been the major cause of poor or low productivity from the forest. But JFM proved that the strict protection which does not need any major investment is good enough to create a good forest. This theory can be best practised specially at ex-zamindary forest of Dhubri Division, where profuse sal natural regeneration is coming out from the copies shoots. Only protection is necessary to establish those seedlings. This can be easily done through the programme of JFM. Social Forestry sector of this distric manages some of the sal forests by giving proper protection and scientific treatment to those area. It is now very encouraging that some of the tribal youths are trying to protect the forest form their core of heart. To get the best result from the JFM, the selected villages should be homogenous, compact and poor. Initially lots of problems may have to be faced by the JFM workers of forest department. But once some cases of success are found then expansion does not have to be faced much problems. However, for this change of mindset, some dedicated forest officer at the helm of affairs must be available. The most important factor of JFM is its continuity. It has been experienced in some states that when a particular officer, who had been in the motivation forces, gets shifted and the new incumbent does not take interest in the programme and ultimately fails it is very difficult and even in some cases, it is next to impossible to revive community participation again once the credibility is lost. It is very common in our villages like others that some of the villagers are closely associated with political parties and group rivalry. In these circumstances, politics and rivalry must be kept away by giving opportunity of participation of all the families in the village. Generally poorest of the poor and women dislike participation in the discussion and planning exercise. It is the duty of the JFM workers to engage those sections of people in all stages of development. The JFM committee should not be viewed only to develop forests but as an instrument for overall development of the village resources and its people. JFM committee should include all age groups of people. In JFM more decision making power should be given to the people by reducing the unilateral powers of the forest officers.

In the seminar "Joint Forest Management scope and potentialities and relevance to Assam" was deliberated on 30th December, 1998 at Assam Forest School, Jalikbari, Guwahati, on the Golden Jubilee of the school Dr. Ajit Kumat Bannerjee, father of JFM, the architect and pioneer of JFM management concept in India and his Arabari (West Bengal) model of 1972 was finally incorporated by the Government of India in the National Forest Policy 1998. It was emphasised that the JFM is the only available handy tools to protect forest and when rural masses are motivated and convinced by the forester then such schemes will definitely succeed. Also, the forester acts as an extension agent and as such, the success story of such project lies in his hands. The innovation and efficiency of a forester plays an important role in JFM to bring the people in close relation with the forestry and environment and its better understanding. In final phase JFM will transfer all forest management to the people and forest officer being used as facilitator in management.

Unemployment is the basic problem now a days specially in Assam. Though the problem of unemployment is common to all countries but the causes and extent may differ from country to country. Under employment is also a problem for society. Unemployment may be internal or external but Assam suffers from external causes of unemployment. Because of advancement in technical skill and highly specialised division of labour, able bodies and capable men are unable to secure jobs. In India, it was estimated that during the third plan period, about 12 million people will be unemployed. To solve this problem the Planning Commission suggested various ways; out of which the development of fisheries and forests was one. The development of forest and fisheries is also to go ahead with development of agriculture. Accordingly, Assam spent Rs. 251 lakhs in forestry sector during IIIrd five year plan. But forestry failed to penetrate the villages of Assam. On the other hand old ponds of villagers were turning into mini fisheries to meet their daily needs of fishes. As the concept of fisheries among the Assamese villagers is not very old, it started since the mid 70 (seventy) of past century. The reasons for non acceptance of forestry by the villagers may be non availability of anything from the surrounding forest or there may be some lacuna among the foresters despite implementing the social forestry project. JFM is the only solution to solve these problems. It will give a gramatic change in unemployment problem for the youth of villages of surrounding forests to provide gainful employment to the rural women and poor masses as everybody knows that scientific management of forests provides more intermediate yield rather than mismanaged forests. Where there is more intermediate yield, there is more income and this income directly goes to the members of the JFM committes besides other income leaving the lions' share of final felling trees.

6

Forest and Panchayat of Assam

"True democracy can not be worked out by twenty persons sitting at the centre. It has to be worked out from below by the people of every village" was the concept of Mahatma Gandhi for the democracy of India. Accordingly, the idea was materialised by incoporating "organization of village panchyats" in the Article 40 of Constitution of India under Directive Principles of State Policy. Prior to this in Assam, the legislation that came into existence was the Rural Panchayati Act, 1948 (Assam Act xvii of 1948) which was passed to establish and develop Local Self Government in the rural areas of the State of Assam and to make better provision for rural administration, reconstruction, and development as self sufficient autonomous units. But after the gap of half a century, the progress and development of Panchayat System in our country is not satisfactory except Maharashtra and Gujrat. In West Bengal, with the active co-operation of Left Front Government, the bonds of the panchayats are becoming more strogner than in past. It will not be enough to speak that the development and progress of Panchayat System in Assam has ended only in casting of votes in ballot boxes. No remarkable development is seen throughout the villages of Assam. Considering the non-development of Panchayat System in India the Janata Government constituted a committee in 1977 to find out the pros and cons of the system headed by Ashok Mehta. This committee recommended two tier Panchayat System instead of three tier as in past. Later on during 1986, Rajiv Gandhi, the then Prime Minister of India formed a committee where L.M.Singhvi was the chairman. With the suggestion of this committee, Rajiv Gandhi Government placed a bill in 1989. Tis bill was defeated in Rajyasabha. Later on, former Prime Minister of India Sri PV.N.S. Roa, again tabled the bill and it was passed in both the houses. This was the 73rd constitution Amendment act, 1992 (The Panchayat Raj) came into effect from 24th April/1993. In view of the constitution, it has become necessary for the Government of Assam to amend and consolidate the laws relating to panchayat in Assam.

Hence, the Government promulgated Assam Panchayat Act, 1994 (Assam Act XVII of 1994) with effect from 5th May/1994 in which a Gaon Panchayat is constituted with population of its territory being not less than six thousand and not more than ten thosand. Even the forest villages and tea garden areas are also within the purview of this act. Major achievement of this act is that not less than one-third of the total number of seats to be filled up by the direct election in every Gaon Panchayat, shall be reserved for women and such seats may by allotted by rotation to different constituencies in the Gaon Panchayat.

Besides other provisions, this act also significantly deals with social forestry of Assam. Under section 19, functions of Gram Panchayat is described and its sub section (v) states as follows :

1) Planting and preservation of trees on the sides of roads and other public land under its control
2) Plantation of fire-wood trees and fodder development.
3) Promotion of farm forestry.
4) Development of social forestry.

Section 49 deals with general functions of Anchalik panchayat and sub-section (ii) runs as follows :

a) Planting and preservation of trees on the sides of roads and other public lands under its control.

b) Fuel plantation and fodder development.

c) Promotion of farms forestry.

Section 90 related with functions and powers of zilla parishad, where sub-section 8 deals with Social Forestry by way of :

1) Organising campaign for tree planting.

2) Planting and maintenance of trees.

Also as per sub-section 10, Zila parishad is liable for the production of minor forest produce and fuel and fodder by :

1) Promotion of social and farm Forestry, fuel plantation and fodder development.

2) Management of minor forest products of the Forest raised in community land.

3) Development of waste land.

Besides these in the Eleventh Schedule of Indian Constitution, social Foresty and farm Forestry is included. Having all these provisions and facilities, the social forestry project of Assam is not acepted by the people upto the mark. Also, it is not so much popular among the villagers. People's interest ends in collection of free distributed seedlings from near by social forestry offices without taking any care for their survival, even sometimes these are not planted in soil also. People think that social forestry means the plantations raised by the Government by encroaching their V.G.R. P.G.R. and other public lands. They never think that the social forestry means for the people and by the people.

Every message of Government specially in the line of development should reach each of the families of the country. There lies the success or failure of the development of the Government. Panchayat Raj system of Assam ought to play the vital role in this matter, besides other Government Departments or agencies related to the rural development. Unfortunately, the Assam Panchayat System has totally failed to serve this purpose.

Role of panchayat in social forestry of Assam is cipher only. In Tamil Nadu earning of panchayat from plantations by harvesting and with sharing with the Government in the ratio of 60:40 is shown below in the following table from 1981 to 1994.

Year	Amount paid to panchayats as 60% share (Rs. in lakhs)	No. of panchayats benefitted
1981-88	431:55	1050
88-89	70:89	237
89-90	196:29	442
90-91	397:54	750
91-92	588:82	788
92-93	365:52	754
93-94	439:67	378

But what about our panchayats? Not a single rupee is earned by planting and selling a single tree within the whole of Assam. The reasons behind this are :-

(1) Due to lack of awareness for tree planting or tree cultivation among the villagers.

(2) As the panchayat members are coming from the elite groups of villagers, they are neither bothered to motivate the villagers to raise plantations nor they are willing to help the poor people of the village to develop tree planting economically in waste land, P.G.R., V.G.R. river bed sides etc.

(3) Panchayat members are losing their capacity (which was there upto seventies) to mobilise the villagers for voluntary participations and to organise for the development of social forestry or other development activities.

(4) Panchayat members are having no deep, concrete thinking for employment generation programme through Agro-Forestry or social forestry projects, like Bee-keeping, wood based cottage industries, fruit processing and preservation industries etc.

All these afflictions of Assam panchayat will evaporate as and when panchayat workers will really work for the interest of the poor villagers. Also when the villagers will know the value of trees, they will surely love the trees. The research of Dr. Tarak Mohan Das of Calcutta University found out the value of a tree and monetary benefits derived from a medium-size tree of 50 tonnes during its span of 50 year as under :

1.	Production of oxygen	=	Rs. 2,50,000.00
2.	Conservation to animal protein.	=	Rs. 20,000.00
3.	Controlling of soil erosion & soil fertility	=	Rs. 2,50,000.00
4.	Recalling of water and controlling of humidity	=	Rs. 3,00,000.00
5.	Sheltering of birds, insects, squirrels & plants	=	2,50,000.00
6.	Controlling of air pollution	=	Rs. 5,00,000.00
	Total	=	**Rs. 15,70,000.00**

But in Assam, from Sodia to Dhubri, medium size tree at current market rate (of timber) would hardly fetch Rs. 5,000.00 which is only 0.3% of the real value of the tree.

Not only the panchayat acts, but also the forestry which was previously in "State List" was included in "concurrent List" after 42nd amendment of the constitution in 1976. Hence, now the constitution recognises the rights of both Parliament and the State Legislatures to legislate concurrently with regard to the forests. Moreover, according to the 42nd amendment, 10 fundamental duties were included for the citizen of India in Indian Constitution. The 7th, fundamental duty for all citizens of India is "to protect and improve natural environment, including forests, lakes, rivers, wild life and have compassion for living creatures". But in reality, these fundamental duties of the citizens are disregarded specially in Assam. We are more conscious of our fundamental rights but not for our fundamental duties. Duties and rights are the two faces of a coin.

India is losing at an alarming rate of 1.5 million hectares of forests annually. " Ultimately environmental deterioration is not merely a case of pollution or of destruction of nature but that the destruction of nature leads to the status of human beings, specially those belonging to the weaker sections also. It is because the weaker sections depend on nature more than others" (Fernandes. W-Forest Environments and People). Hence, to survive the mankind specially the nature dependent poor sections of the people, they have to protect and preserve the forests and trees, for their own interests. These problems have to be realised by the villagers of Assam. Panchayats of Assam should take a programme for massive tree planting through voluntary labour to solve the various burning problems of the state. We can have experienced from the family planning programme. Family planning programme takes more or less twenty years to reach the present stage but the massive tree planting scheme surely does not requires so much of time because family planning is more private and individualistic, whereas tree planting is a social and religious programme. Assam panchayat has to play the role of axle of the vehicle to implement the scheme of tree planting or tree cultivation for the better development of poor villages within the state. So, at the very dawn of 21st century (As presently panchayat election is not held) 78438 sq. km. geographical area of Assam having 23 districts, 2486 Gaon Panchayats and 25596 villages (As per 1991 census) will be prosperous with the help of panchayats in all angles of development particularly by tree planting and protecting the trees for the betterment of the poor villages. Panchayat should adhere to the basic function of Gaon Sabha or Gaon Panchayat and mobilize voluntary labour for developmental work failing which, the whole concept of Gandhiji's dream will be frustrated.

7
ANCIENT FOREST AND WILD LIFE

The relationship between 'M', and 'N' is very close to each other. Man can not survive alone without nature. Nature is a composition of many more ingredients like soil, water, air, minerals etc. Forest which includes plant and animal kingdom is one of the major ingredients of nature. This was clearly understood by our forefathers more than us they were more close to forests. So they were knew more about forest than we know now. Assam forests contains more than 22,000 plant species, out of which presently we know hardly 2% of them for their utilization. Many descriptions of forest, trees and wild animals are found in ancient literatures. Worship of tree was extended through out the world in ancient times. Traces of this are still found in many places. Worship of tree was seen in India during Mohenjodro civilization which was excavated by Rakhal Das Bandhopadhyaya in 1922 and in Harappa civilization whose excavation was led by Daya Ram Shahani during 1921.

Bamboo is very common to all specially for Assamese Society. The origin of bamboo is found in PURANA, where it describes that Murala was a Brahmin girl who was married to a Shudra without her knowledge. But after knowing that, Murala prepared her pyre and prayed Vishnu to die. She died and from the ashes of Murala, the bamboos were grown; the bamboo is the symbol of fire. The friction of dry bamboos create fire inside forest as believed by our ancestors.

Kautilaya's Arthashastra is one of the excellent works on royal ethics even for forest and wild life. Kautilaya described that not less than 100 families and not more than 500 families should constitute a village and the boundary should be well demarcated by planting simal or ficus trees. Felling of such trees was punishable. This practice is still prevailing more or less in the villages of Assam by planting trees on the boundaries of home state lands. Also, a large flat forest area consists of tasty edible fruits and thornless trees should be kept reserved for recreation of kings. The same idea is prevailing still today. So, to get the recreational value from forest, it is one of the objects for preservation and conservation of sanctuary, National parks etc besides others. Specific mandatory rules were strictly imposed for shouting as warning to run away during the time of felling trees. This logging rule is practised in modern times also. Teak, Aurjuna, Sal, Sissoo, etc. were treated as valuable forest produces. Felling of trees without paying tax was punishable except to escape from danger.

Elephant was part and parcel in battles during the ancient times. So, the kings were compelled to maintain large number of elephants to be used in different battles. Kautilaya elaborately described different aspects of elephants. Such as elephant of Kalinga was best in quality and elephant of Sourashtra was worst. Summer season was the best season for elephant capturing. Twenty years old elephant was fit for capture. Suckling, ill-health pregnant elephant was unfit for capture. Rice, oil, ghee, salt, sugarcane-juice, alcohol, green fodder, etc. was to be supplied as food to each of captive elephant in different ratio depending upon the height of the elephant. Supply of green leaves was unlimited.

Elephants were classified into four classes (1) Fit for training, (2) Fit for battle, (3) Fit for riding and (4) Mad elephant. The following acts were punishable and fines were collected out of food allowances and salaries from the officer incharge of elephant :

(1) kept unclean areas where elephants are kept.

(2) Non supply of food in appropriate quantities and qualities.

(3) Compelled the elephant to sleep in barren land during night time.

(4) Hurt the elephant at delicate point of the body.

(5) Allow ride to unauthorised persons.

(6) Compelled the elephant to cross the thick forest or jungle.

Elephant tusk should be cut at the interval of two and a half years for the elephant grazing at alluvial soil of river banks and at the gap of five years for hilly elephant. Elephant tusk was to be cut above the height of double of the circumstance at the collar. During Maurya period, some villages were registered as free of tax but those villagers had to supply fixed quantities of different forest produced to the king. Even sometimes forest produced were given to the officers as salaries in lieu of cash money when there was shortage of money in treasury. Separate godown was created for storage of forest products. Authorised persons of civil administration were entrusted to control and supervise the forest and forest produces, and to collect revenue from them. Not going further, it can be concluded that during Maurya period the management of forest was well developed in India as found in the Arthshastra of Kautilya. Ashok introduced the tree planting on road side and now this is accepted by modern forest management practice in India.

In Harmohon part of Kirtan of Sankardev (1449-1568) the names of many trees are found. Some of which are palash, paruli, Bakul, Kadam, Nageswar, Champa, Madar etc. Also in Gajendra fabliau of the same epic, the names of Ashok, Am, Jam, Agar, Sonaru etc were mentioned. Besides, all these medicinal values of trees were known to all since time immemorial. Even in modern computerised age also, large number of medicines are extracted from plant kingdom. Many life saving drugs are prepared from plants. Ayurveda shastra is mostly related with drugs prepard from plant kingdom and it is the origin of medical science.

In Ahom period of Assam, though the revenue was paid terms of personal service (paik system) gradually, the demand of cash money made it necessary to realise revenue in cash. Hence, at the later period, an alternative arrangement was made for the payment of revenue in cash if a paik failed to render personal service to the state. Also, a large amount of cash money was realised as royalties paid for cutting timbers, penalties for theft etc. Ahoms, kept some areas as 'jhangal bhumi' (Forest land) which were not considered for revenue purposes unless they were cleared by the people and were included in the land survey. The other category of land "Habipitani" found in the grant of Gouri Nath Singh, stands for watery region covered with forest. Ahom Kings were allowed free use of trees in the waste lands, but after the British annexation even the owners of the Muga silk products grown in the forests were compelled to pay revenue for their use of the forest lands, causes of destruction of forests of Assam starts from the days of the British. Also large tracts of forest areas were cleared for tea gardens. Even those waste lands were placed under the class of rent free land. In that case, Powell's view was – "That an immense tract of jungle lands could best be utilised to the advantages of the people and the state by bringing them under cultivation of tea but it is not at all commendable, for we have seen that at the cost of Assam and her poor people, the individual tea gardens and the company derived enormous profit". This system ultimately creates "Planters' Raj" wing of British Imperialism within Assam. Today also, in our independent country; Assam Panchayat Raj is mere spectator of Planters' Raj. No fruits of Assam

Panchayat Raj are germinated within the jurisdiction of Planters' Raj.

History says that, King Rudra Singha constructed the first Rang-Ghar to enjoy sports by sal posts. The description of workmanship of Ahom city by Persian historian Shihabuddin Talish was "My pen fails to describe in detail the other arts and rare inventions employed in decorating the wood work of this place (Garhgaon). Probably nowhere else in the whole world can wooden houses be built with such decoration and figure carving as by the people of this country." The precious wood works during Ahom period was only possible due to the availability of trees and timbers. Ahom prepared bridges by boats during wars. Even the source of income of religious institution like Satras and temples were consisted of sale proceeds of valuable trees like sals and Bansoms of the allowed lands. For example, the endowments granted to Madhaba temple of Hajo consisting of 54253 Bighas and 4 kathas of land including forests and fisheries continue upto the year 1904.

Ahom kings were also very fond of elephants like others. The great work of "Hastirvirdarnav" was completed by Sukumar Borkath during the time of Siva Singh. King Pratap Singha was interested in elephant capturing. He had decided to capture one thousand elephants and accordingly he did it. Then he got the title of Gajapati, the owner of one thousand elephants. After this, in 1625 he established a new town named as Gajpur, which is presently situated towards eastern side of Jorhat town. Many old villages were found by the names of trees within Assam, some of which are Jamuguri, Simlaguri, Bagribari, Kathalguri etc.

No such precious works were found during Mughal period of India for the interest of forest and wild life. As most of the Mugal kings were busy in various battles for their establishment and to extend their territory within India. However, Mughal gardens in India are one of the important development of forestry. Gardens were popular in Iran. Babar transplanted his love for them into Indian soil. Remnants of his Aram Bagh or garden are still in Agra. Gardens were included in all Mughal palaces and tombs and were laid out purely for enjoyment. Shahjahan completed his Shalimar gardens in Lahore (Pakistan) in 1637. Fountain normally featured in these gardens as the Mughals were seeking shelter from the heat and dust of Hindustan.

The name of the place Bhomoraguri is known to all Assamese people. Probably the area of Bhomoraguri was full of Bhomora tree (*Terminalia bellerica*) in past, but it related to the histroy of Assam. In 1795 at Kamrup, Har Dutta and Bir Dutta the two brothers started revolution against the King Kamaleshwar Singha. This is known "Dhandua Drah" in Assam history. Barphukan Kalia Bhomora controlled this rebel and he obtained the name Pratap Ballav. This Barphukan was started to construct a wooden bridge on Brahmaputra at the site of the present Kalia Bhomra bridge whose foundation was laid by the then Prime Minister of India, Morarji Desai on 2nd November 1978. Barphukan Pratap Balav collected the sal posts from the forest of north bank of Mara Bharulu river and trasported through Bharulu river to the site of the proposed bridge. The remains of those sal posts were found still 1978 as mentioned by Sri Jiban Das, a Retd. Forest Officer of Assam. (Assam Bani 18-12-1978, Letters to the Editor). Evidence states that late Ratana Bahadur Katel, inhabitant of Bhomoraguri construnted his own double storeyed building from the timbers collected and stored by Kaliabhomora for the purpose of construction of bridge upon mighty Brahamaputra linking Silghat and Bhomoraguri. Ratana Bahadur Katel died in 1941 at the age of 108 years. (Dainik Assam 2-11-1978 Narendra Dev Sastri). The venture of construction a bridge upon Brahamaputra remained incomplete due to his sudden death.

Development of wood works and availability of timbers could be easily imagined from those activities in past. But now we are in shortage of timbers. At present, our wooden bridges remain unrepaired for the non-availability of timbers. If the time passes like wise, our carpenters, wood workers etc. will automatically lose their efficiency; their instruments will be blunt. A clear example is the ivory industry of Assam which reached the Zenith during Ahom period. Leaving other products of ivory in olden days, even the fans ware prepared and presented to many Kings by the Ahom kings as a token of friendship. But at present, the whole industry has become decrepit.

Summarising all this, it is true that our forests in ancient times were very luxurious. Kings protected the forest and people loved forest for their own interest. Forest were reduced due to increase in population specially in Assam and their unlimited needs. From the records, it is revealed that in 1769-70, the population of undivided Assam was estimated at about 2.5 million and now it comes to 22,414,322 (1991 census). "The steady increase in population, towards the close of our period, was due to natural growth under settled condition and mainly due to the influax of outsiders nearly 65 per cent of Bengal, 14 per cent from united provinces and 10.8 per cent from the central provinces" (Assam in the days of the company - H.K. Borpujari). Population increase can not be a major factor for the destruction of nature as well as forests and trees. Citizen should be conscious and conservative in utilisation of natural resources. Forests and trees are renewable natural resource. So if we felled one tree and we plant two trees we will get double in future. We can easily create more than 22 million trees in a single day within Assam if we implement the slogan – "A plant for a person", then only we will get the forest of our past and be able to handover a green Assam to our next generation for their future benefits and thus we can prove "Man is the nature's mistake" (Gillbert) is wrong.

8

Terrorist and Joint Forest Management of Assam

Terrorism is the systematic violence in the furtherance of political aims, often caused by small guerrila groups. It is a specific social phenomenon, has a describable origin and predictable end. If we turn the pages of history of Russisa, the 'Nihilist Movement' will attract our eyes and brain. Nihilist member was of a group of Russian revolutionaries in the reign of Alexander II (1855 to 81). The name popularised by the writer Turgenev, means one who approves of nothing (Latin NIHIL) and belonging to the existing order. In 1878, the Nihilists launched a guerrilla compaign leading to the murder of the Tsar in 1881. The Nihilist were stern materialists. For them, "Shoe maker was more useful than one who was a Shakesperean scholar". In support of this movement at Russia, Belinsky remarked, "people have a need for potatoes but not least for a constitution." Nihilist movement was crushed by iron handed repression and the Nihilist also failed to enlist mass support for them.

Terrorism is familier to Indian culture, including the freedom struggle also. During Freedom movement, they felt that violence was the only method by which they could turn out the British from the Indian soil. They believed that nothing could be achieved by constitutional methods and knew that freedom could not be achieved unless they took the arms. For terrorist activities, the name of 'Masterda', Surya Sen is found in the history of East Bengal, who was the leader of terrorists groups at that time. Hem Chandra, a terrorist and zeolous patriot went to France to learn the art of manufacturing explosives. Aswini Kumar Dutta, Jatindranath Mukharjee, Narendra Nath Dutta etc, organised the young men so that they could carry on a revolutionary struggle. On 6th Dec 1907, a train in which is Lt. Governor was travelling, was blown up by the terrorist near Midnapore. Allan, an Ex-Disrict Magistrate of Dhaka faced terrorist attack at Faridpur Railway station. Also an attempt was made on the life of King Ford, the judge of Muzaffarpur on 30th, April, 1908. The Deputy Superintendent of police was shot dead in front of the Calcutta High Court on 24th, January 1910. Sir Curzen wyllie, political adviser to the secretary of state for India, was shot-dead at the doorsteps of his office in London by an Indian Patriot, Madanlal Dhingra on 1st July 1909.

In Assam also on 26th February 1857, the hanging of Maniram Dewan and Pyali Barua was carried out. The death sentences was passed in the court of Deputy Commissioner, Sibsager, Mr. Holroyod. Jeuram Duila and Pyali Borphukan were sentenced to death by Captain Neufville and David Scot approved the sentence of hanging. In August 1830, the execution of order against thse two patriots was carried out in Sibsagar. On the 4th April 1829, Tirot Sing, a Khasi rebellion, the chief of Nongkhalow killed two British officers Bultron and Bedings and fled along with sixty Indian sepoys. At last, in January 1833, Tirot Sing surrendered and the rebelion was over, and the Khasi hills passed under the British rule. Kanoklata, the first Indian lady of Assam sacrificed her life for the country in front of the bullets of British at Gahpur police station.

Moamaria rebellion (1769) during Ahom peirod of Assam also may be classfied under terrorist activities. Though some of the historian placed this revolution under peasant revolution and some believe that it was a conflict between the Sakta and Vaishnava.

In January 1794, captain Welsh set forth with Gaurinath Singh on his march against the Mamorias. Gaurinath Singh undertook to pay a sum of Rs. 3,00,000 (Rupees three lakh) annually for the maintenance of the British troops in Assam. Numerous Mamorias were killed by captain Welsh and the rebellion thus came to an end. 'Dundua Droh' was also one terrorist movement in Assam histroy which is mentioned in our ancient forest and wild life"

Climbing the historical leader of terrorism the last two decades of 20th century, every centimetre of Assam experienced with terrorist activities. Not only in Assam but all the North Eastern States of India are tasting the same fruit juice. During September 1979, All Assam Student Union (AASU) and All Assam Gana Sangram Parisad (AAGSP) started the peaceful, non-violent movement for detection and deportation of all the foreign infiltrators from Assam. They demanded that for detection and deportation of the foreigners, illegally staying in Assam, the National Register of Citizens (N.R.C.) 1951, which is based on the relevant sections of the Constitution of India and derived from the 1951 census, must be made the basis. Also, the person covered by the Nehru-Liaquat Pact 1950 are to be accommodated (person coming to India before 31.12.50 became an Indian citizen). This agitation not only has the sanction of the people of Assam but also has support of the indigenous people of all sister states of North East Region. The problem of foreign infiltration into Assam was reflected in official records also. "A large number of outsiders mostly from East Bengal began to pour in large numbers into Assam from the beginning of the present century". (Assam Land Revenue Manual, Vol. 1, 7th edition 1956). In 1901, Assam was linked by railways with the other parts of the country and a special train was operated from Mymensingh in East Bengal to Moirabari in Nowgong with a view to changing the character, composition and demographic change of the local Assamese society. In October 1938, Lokopriya Gopinath Bordoloi formulated a new land settlement policy with active co-operation of Rupnath Brahma. It was laid down that and East Bengal Muslim arriving in Assam later than 31.12.1937, shall not be entitled to settle in Assam. The Bordoloi Ministry resigned on December 1941 as suggested by Mahatma Gandhi and Sir Mohammed Sadulla took the charge of the Government and he initiated two programmes, the development scheme and the colonisation scheme. Large number of migrant muslims from East Bengal were settled at Barpeta, Nowgaon and Mongaldoi District in the name of grow more food campaign. Question of present Dhubri district (Now a portion of old Goalpara District) was out of question as it was and is the gate way of migrants to Assam. After independence, East Bengal formed part of a foreign country viz. Pakistan and styled as East Pakistan and large number of refugees came to Assam and Tripura. This led to an alarming situation and the Government of India introduced a Bill in the Parliament on 24.12.1949 which was "The immigrants, (Expulsion from Assam Act, 1950". The statement of objects and reasons said,"During the last few months, a serious situation has arisen from the immigration of a very large number of East Bengal residents into Assam". Such large migration is disturbing the economy of the province, besides giving rise to a serious law and order problems". Sec. 2 of this act found that the stay of such persons or class of persons of Assam is detrimental to the interests of the general public of India or of any section there of or of any Scheduled Tribe in Assam". With the help of the Immigrants Act, 1950, Government of Assam under the leadership of the then Home Minister Bishnu Ram Medhi started detection and deportation of the foreigners but Pakistan complained about it. Then Pandit Jawaharlal Nehru and Md. Liaquat

Ali Khan sat on a discussion which ended on 6.4.1950 by signing the Nehru-Liquat Pact, and on 17.9.1957, The Immigrants (Expulsion from Assam) Act 1950 was repealed. In 1961, Census estimated that the minimum of 7.50 lakhs of East Pakistan Muslims entered Assam illegally and the then Prime Minister of India in 1956 made a statement in Lok Sabha for this problem. However, B.P. Chaliha, the then Chief Minister of Assam estimated the influx of about 3.5 lakhs and arrangements were made to expel the Pak Muslim infiltraters from Assam. Accordingly, 1.92 lakh infiltrators were expelled and deported during 1967 to 1969. As the process was continuing, 33 Congress Legislators, (Assam) headed by Mainul Haque Choudhury, Dev Kanta Baruah and Sarat Chandra Singha revolted against the action of the Government and the entire process of detection and deportation was ended. After the formation of Bangladesh, the then Prime Minister of India, Indira Gandhi and the then Prime Minister of Bangladesh, Sheikh Mujibur Rehman came to a pact that the East Pakistanis who illegally entered into India before 25.3.1971 shall not be deported, and accordingly, the Minister of Home Affairs, Government of India, vide Memo no. 11/160/72-Tx dated 30.9.1972 advised the State Government of Assam.

In 1931 C.S. Mullan in his census report said "That in another 30 years Sibsagar District will be the only part of Assam in which an Assamese will find himself at home". The prediction of Mullan came to the reality which is found in the following table.

During discussion of foreigner national at Rajya Saba in 1964, the then Rajya Sabha M.P. from Assam, Baharul Islam, the Retired Chief Justice, Guwahati High Court, said that the Pakistani National who were in Assam without any valid authority, must be evicted from the country. What the Government of India is doing, they are approaching the problems in a very human manner.

Population Figures or 1951, 1961 and 1971

State and Districts	1951	1961	Percentage of increase	1971	Percentage of increase
1	2	3	4	5	6
Assam	8,028,856	10,837,329	34.98	14,625,152	34.95
Kamrup	1,490,329	2,062,572	38.40	2,854,183	38.33
Goalpara	1,108,124	1,543,892	39.32	2,225,103	44.12
Nowgaon	886,955	1,210,761	36.51	1,680,895	38.83
Darrang	923,562	1,289,670	39.64	1,736,188	34.62
Sibsagar	1,212,224	1,508,390	24.43	1,837,389	21.81
Lakhimpur	1126,294	1,563,842	38.84	2,122,719	35.71
United Mikir & North Cachar Hills	165,440	279,726		455,357	62.79
Cachar	1,115,865	1,378,476	23.53	1,713,318	24.29

Firstly, the Pakistani nationals were served with notices and then they were given some time to quit although there is no provision in the foreigner's act for giving notice to the Pakistani nationals. They simply may be arrested and then evicted." (Assam Information, Govt. of Assam, 1964, Vol. XV. No. 8)

G.L. Nanda, the then Home Minister of India in March 1964, addressed a Public Meeting and said "Illegal infiltrants must leave India" and at a press conference at the Borjhar Airport he said "We talk of Pakistani infiltrants; we talk of foreigners and not of India Muslim". Also he said at Shillong that the security of the country is threatened and the people of Assam and Khasi and Jaintia Hill districts have a very important responsibility to discharge in defending the country from foreign aggression."

In 1961-1971 census population of Assam increased by 34.94% against the national rise of 24.94% and during 1951-61 growth of population was 34.99% (say 35%) against national increase of 21.64%. During 1951-61, the increase population in Tripura was 78.71%, Manipur 35.04% and during 1961-71, the increase of population at Nagaland was 39.85% (say 40%). Arunachal Pradesh was also not lagging behind as its curves read 38.91% (say 39%) increase of population during 1961-71. From these figures, everybody can realise why the names of Assam, Manipur, Nagaland and Tripura are printed on headlines of all newspapers of India even abroad, since last two decades of 20th Century. Vested interest even today are trying to ignore the problem or minimise its magnitude, a problem which to-day is striking at the very core of the states demographic, ethnic and socio-economic structure. There is a wrong notion in other parts of India that there is plenty of cultivable waste land in Assam. But in fact, no land is available at present. As in the year 1951, the per capita agriculture land in the State was 0.36 hectare, in 1961 it became 0.27 hectare, in 1971 it decreased to 0.2 hectare and in 1980 it has come down to 0.14 hectare. In this context the statement of a U.N. demographer may be mentioned, "there would be only standing room for every man within 800 yards if the present rate of growth of population continues".

No one could clearly define what is terrorism and what is insurgency. Political scholars also do not have one voice. Even the UNO has also failed to find out an agreeable definition on terrorism and insurgency. But every body will accept that it is a social problem and clearly a social disorganization for a given period. M.A. Elliot and F.E. Merrill rightly said that "social disorganization represents a breakdown in the equilibrium of forces, a decay in the social structure, so that old habits and forms of social control no longer function effectively." (Cultural Sociology 1951, p. 740). Assamese social structure is decaying, Assamese social functions are not effective at all, within Assam and all social structure of all indigenous communities is decaying. All social function of all sons of soil are not functioning effectively at all. Bartrand Russell observes that the lack of adjustment in institutions based on authority in the past is responsible for present social disorganisation. This very truth is totally applicable for the social disorganisation of Assam and N.E. regions of India social problem in various fields such as economic, philosophy, political science, sociology etc. are considered to be the symptoms of social disorganisation. For example unemployment in the economic field, political corruption in the political field were considered to the problems threatening the smooth working of the society. These social problems were considered to be the diseases of the society, which threatened the welfare of the society. The society could progress only when these disease were removed or in other words, these social problems were solved. This requires some sort of collective action. When an individual (or a group of individuals) is disorganised and is not functioning according to the norms laid down by the society, the social problems continue to exist. It can be verified from the speech of Sri Ramendra Narayan Kalita, Handloom Textiles and Sericulture Minister of Assam while addressing a meeting held on 31st December 1999 at Rani Development Block office premises "The youth should give up the gun culture and inculcate the habit of work culture. Gun culture can in no way develop a nation. It is only the work culture that makes a nation developed in all spheres. To-day the youth in Assam are inculcating the habit of gun culture for the step motherly treatment of the Central Government". (The Assam Tribune 11th January, 2000). From this, every body can easily imagine the extent of decay of societies within Assam, and how much social control is functioning. The picture is almost more or less similar throughout the whole North-East regions. Assam is not poor but the Assamese are poor. Assamese means all communities of sons soil. Assam produces 50 per cent mineral oil of India (4838000

M.T. during 1991). But Guwahati Refinery refined only 0.75 M.T. and Bongaigaon refinery produces 1.00 M.T. where as Barauni refinery gives final products of 3.00 M.T. whose crude oil is supplied through the world's longest pipeline from Assam. Assam having 848 tea gardens covering 229428 hect. of area which yeilds 3798500 kg of tea and an average 1656 kg per hect., while the country is having 13853 tea gardens who produce 688105000 kg only (Statistical Handbook Assam 1993). Assam is one of the largest jute producing state of India. In Assam 102000 hect. area produced 867000 tonnes of jute during 1992. Assam gives 982000 M.T. coal to the nation and 268000 M.T. of lime stone was produced during 1991. The mighty river Brahmaputra is capable to produce 12000 M.W. electricity annually but it generates only 1086.3 M.W. The per capita consumption of electricity is only 64 K.W. during 1995. Also, as per 1991 census only, 21481 villages were electrified out of total 25590 villages of Assam. The length of N.F. Railway is 3858 km. out of which Assam was having only 2467 km. upto 1995. Likewise, lots of datas can be quoted. But from the one can easily understand why the sons of the soil of Asssm are poor. The social problem is rightly observed by Narottam Gaon who writes that "if the influx is not stopped, there will be a sharp decline in communal harmony and the centre-state relations will be vitiated giving rise to separatist tendencies and ethnic crisis in the North Eastern Part of India on a scale larger than what is seen at present". By killing human bodies, the problems of N.E. States can never be solved. For example, from 1996 to the end of 20th century *i.e.* upto 31st December 1999 total 1452 persons were killed within Assam due to terrorist activities, out of which 320 were security personnel, and the balance 1132 were the sons of the soil. But this provides nothing except fuel to the fire. This process can not change the economy of the region which developed as a result of the colonial commercial interests only.

Myron Wiene, rightly observed, that the presence of immigrants shook the foundation of Assamese social structure and created solidarity among Assamese and Tribals, (sons of the soil, migration and ethnic conflicts on India) because in the North East of India, every sub-division or district (civil) has the inherent contradiction of a polyglot society.

Presently "there is no development as Central Government does not provide fund for development." This sentence is echoing at the air of N.E. Regions, specially within Assam. No doubt, it is a serious problem but according to B.B. Kumar the actual problem lies in misutilization and drainage of funds, politicization of development resources and lack of financial discipline which are the root causes for non-development. Also he said "The tendency to blame other for every ill of the society is a dangerous sysmptom. It creates ideal environment for insurgent activities." (Insurgency in North-East India.). Sanjoy Hazorika writes "local need to be given effective control over resources, and development schemes must have their participation and not be devised and dictated by central authorities." (Insurgency in N.E. India). No one should forget that the extremists may be the enemies of the King/Government/or Authorities." But they are really more patriotic than you and me. As they are patriots they surely love the natural resources but the natural resources must be used for the benefits of the common people. They may not like one forester but they never dislike any forests. For example, some extremist groups at present protect some of the forests of Dhubri Forest Division very nicely. Even many wood cutter's lives were withdrawn by the bullets of these extremist groups. Remarkably all the dead bodies of wood cutters were from the immigrant class. Not a single dead body was identified as the sons of the soil, neither Hindus nor Muslims. If the milk of forests can be drunk equally by the sons of the soil who lives within or on the periphery of forests, why they will kill this cow (forests)? Rather, they will nourish. But if the milk of forests is pumped to Delhi, Patna, Calcutta etc., by totally depriving the youth the sons of the soil, why they will not cry or not become angry? Remembering this, all Foresters starting from the forest guards now try to give shares of benefits of forest to the villagers specially living within or around the forest. Simply notification, no. FRW 8/93/75 dated 10th November 1998. (The Assam Joint People's Participation Forestry Management Rules 1998) issued by the Government of Assam will serve nothing. (Details of the notification are given in the later part of this book). It is a fact that the forest personnel of Assam are now frustrated, with the old systems of forest management. They are simply working for the Government but not for the common people. This frustration will end only when the forest personnel start working for the interest of both the Government and the common people. Forest Department of Assam should act as the nodal agency in planning various activities for integrated rural development; specifically within or just around the forest areas. This is possible only through Joint Forest Management system which must improve the overall quality of life. J.F.M.'s aim is not to encourage Government programmes alone where the villagers become passive beneficiaries. They must be encouraged to stand on their own feet. If the J.F.M. system carried out successfuly, the scheme could also steam the trend of urban drift from villages. With the gradual strengthening of the economy, villagers would become more receptive to health care, ecology, education and small savings etc. eventually being able to take a decision for improving their lot. In fact, a strong village economy may also initiate the phenomenon of "Rural Drift" from urban centres. J.F.M. system may not sprinkle sufficient water in the fire of insurgency problem of Assam, but it will surely spray atleast few drops of dew, at the very dawn of 21st.

century. In Assam cultivated area is only 34%. Hence there are ample areas, ever ready to accept the J.F.M. such as river side areas, water logged low lying areas, char areas etc. and the programme can be introduced so that the available lands can be utilised rationally. If this can be materialised, then probably the bullets of the terrorist will aim at the water currents of mightly Brahmaputra only; not for others. If the sons of the soil of Assam get 'potato' they can stand on their own legs and their hands can be engaged at income generating (Productive) purposes then where they will loss their identity. But for this situation, a sincere and honest team is necessary which should consist of politicians, Government machinery and noble sons of the soil.

9

J.F.M. AND MOTIVATION

Joint Forest Management (J.F.M.) is presently, a well accepted and approved system of management of forests with the help of local people. But to start or switch on this JFM system many hurdles have to be crossed specially the motivation. It should be remembered that 'motivation is power'. No one is clear, as to how exactly the motivation works and influence human behaviour as motivators are varied and powerful. They change from time to time. Motives are five fingers–1. Achievement, 2. Pestise, 3. Security, 4. Money and 5. Affiliation.

Achievement motives is the desire to reach for something better than the individual already has, but achievement is a personal matter. It gives a person something he can get, in no other way. In J.F.M. system, the motivators have to hammer the participants in this track as the participants will get the following benefits –

(1) 25% output from silviculture thinning beside other 'usufructs' benefits.

(2) 25% from main fellings.

As per the provision of the Assam Joint (people's participation) Forestry Management Rules 1998 under Rule 10(iii) & IV, People accept challenges if the achievement motive is rooted in their brain, and this is the duty of the motivators mainly the forest personnels.

In J.F.M. motivation programme, the recognition of achievement oriented persons is very essential.

1. An achievement oriented person is aware of his obstacles but not worried by them.
2. He pours his entire resources into gaining success.
3. He accepts challenges no matter what the obstacle is?
4. He move where angles fairs to tread?
5. He likes to win.
6. He likes tasks and getting jobs done where there is a possibility of risk and failure but it is not too great.

In P.R.A. for J.F.M. conversation with the people is main ingredient. We remember that conversation is a vehicle to convey understanding, education, experience and much more. It is an efficient method of social intercourse in which people get to know each other, conversation is right when motivators are not monopolizing it. J.F.M. workers determine the people's likes, their wants, problems and not just the interests but their pride. Encourage people to talk, let them express their ideas and opinions. Please them by asking their advice. A successful motivator always suggests the following :

1. Never gossip. Smile gently,
2. Recognise that the other person has feelings,
3. Recognise that he has an opinion,
4. Give him a chance to voice his opinion,
5. Never challenge others' self respect,
6. Walk way from all hight tension problems,
7. Be generous, be charitable.
8. Be courageous,
9. Talk only good things, avoid the bad and unfavourable.

10. Retain high level honesty.
11. Praise people lavishly.
12. Be sincere.
13. Give freely to those who need your help.
14. Never discredit anyone or speak disparagingly.
15. Say nothing detrimental about any one who is absent.

Religion and politics are never discussed by the J.F.M. motivators and bad social habits of other should be avoided during discussion or in public gathering.

Most of the J.M.F. workers or forest officers are facing lots of problems to handle arguments and to handle irate people. There is no one way to handle it. There are many ways, and these should be fitted to the situation and circumstances. Some of them are :

1. Tell him he is perfectly right, agree with him, which will stop him going cold? Give him attention and not an argument.
2. Permit him to deliver his tirade unopposed "would you please repeat it so that I can understand just a little bit better". This type of request will evaporate the anger of the person. So be diplomatic in such condition.
3. Walk away from argument.
4. Never argue, no argument is ever logical. Be lavish with praise. Say to that person, Friend! that is good idea. I would never have thought of it.
5. Never permit emotion to influence you, in such circumstances simply provide no fuel for others to burn.
6. Forget remarks designed to "cut somebody down" – Be kind.

Be sympathetic. Be understanding. Later, one can get the social problem under control through diplomacy.

7. If you have been insulted, forget it.
8. Accept criticism easily.
9. Never critise.
10. Walk and talk softly in the state of anger, keep in mind that your point of view is no interest to him.
11. Answer all questions with more questions.
12. Let him know that you understand.
13. Get close to him. Look at him in the eyes.
14. Talk in the language he understands and only what he knows.
15. Keep self interest out; refuse to be selfish, see the entire picture; Act for the benefit of the majority.
16. Listen! adopt the other person's ideas.
17. Co-operate.
18. Keep positive at all time Expresss nothing negative at any time.
19. Never ask people to do something; do not demand.

Assam forest suffers from bad exposures, means a "poor human relation" or it may be interpreted as "bad publicity" or as "inadequate public relations". Remember humour is strong social control, it often saves a situation when nothing else works.

No success comes without errors and no successful man has ever been free of failure. This established truth can not be ignored bythe J.F.M. workers of Assam. To be a successful J.F.M. worker, the 4.D.S. will guide the right path. These are Determination, Decision, Design and

Distribution. In J.F.M. gatherings, mainly the following points are to be touched :

1. Touch the emotion of participants.
2. Touch the vanity of participants.
3. Touch the hopes and prayers of participants.
4. Touch the pride of participants.

Psychotherapist, Dr. George Weinberg says –

Force a man to fight for a issue, and if he manages to survive, he'll believe in that issue more strongly than he did. Hence force the participants by way of motivation to fight for J.F.M and support to manage to survive. Then he will believe in JFM more strongly than the past Conventional System of Forest Management. For this, treat the people with kindness; continue to respect them and enjoy their company. But be careful not to allow people to mistreat you even if they love you. Try to be alert to others people's feelings, Paranoid is a prevalent illness in our society and it is prevalent among people exploited in actuality J.F.M. workers should be able to cure this mental illness of our society and the society should be motivated that J.F.M. system will not exploit them in future as it is just opposite to the past system of Forest Management. It should be borne in mind that directions and orders alone never ensure J.F.M. to get successful results instead the participants are to be motivated. Human mind has to be motivated to think and give their best. Inspire a team spirit in the group and motivate them to realise their sense of responsibility and make them put their joint efforts. In J.F.M. motivation is a process of inspiration to enable members of the group to combinedly carry out the challenge that group has accepted to achieve the goal. But in actual practice in field, it is not so easy. Mistakes, wrong directives, lack of co-ordination, defective planning, communication short falls, groupism, misunderstanding, professional jealousy etc. are common to any organised activity which keeps the task away from getting accomplished.

Motivation is a psychic phenomenon which is exceedingly complex one. It can be better described through a classification of psychic phenomenon and its functioning (see Fig.)

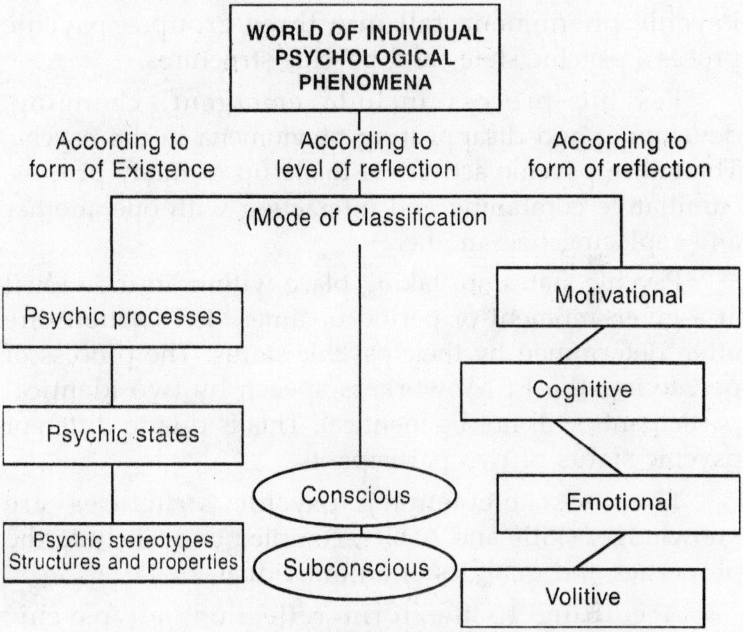

Diagram of Principal Individual Psychological Phenomena Affecting Management

The conscious level of the psychic consciousness is the highest level of reflection and inherent in this level are the psychic phenomena in terms of which man's surrounding are understood, as well as his ego, intentions and relations are known and through which goal-formation, planning and self-control are implemented. Psychological science is now mostly concerned with this highest level of human activity.

The lowest level of the psyche is the subconscious one. In this phenomenon man takes no cognizance of the actions performed, of orientation in the environment, of the motivation and goals of his acts. Sub conscious phenomena in their primary characteristics, are also determined by social conditions, functioning as partial and insufficiently precise reflection of the surroundings. Psychic phenomena fall into three groups– psychic process, psychic states and psychic structures.

Psychic process include emergent, changing, developing and disappearing phenomena in the psyche. The entire psychic activity is made up of many process, cumulative combining and interacting with one another and replacing one another.

Psychic states are taking place within an individual at a given moment or period or time. Men's actions are often determined by their psychic status. The process of perceiving the J.F.M. workers speech by two identical participants will not be identical. This is due to different psychic status of two participants.

The most elementary psychic structures are knowledge, skills and habits, complex ones include the properties and qualities of an individual.

According to the form reflection, all psychic phenomena are divided into four forms - i.e. motivational, cognitive, volitive and emotional. Out of which motivational psychic phenomenon is very important to the J.F.M. Workers.

Motivational psychic phenomena is most important phenomena exerting the strongest influence on all others. Directing motivational phenomena is a most necessary psychological task of any administrator in any directive action. In the absence of suitable motivation of the subordinates, no tasks can be solved.

As the J.F.M. workers mainly work with the groups of people's the study of socio-psychological phenomenon of the particular group is necessary. The past and future of a community group affects their present day psychology. The ideas and views of groups are influenced by traditions, customs, experiences, and memories events of the recent past.

Men's need are varied and may be classified according to a number of criteria. Most frequently, two kinds of such criteria are singled out - Material (the needs for food, water, clothes, housing etc.) and spiritual or social. Needs are formed throughout one's life. Satisfying a need is experienced by man as pleasure, and joy. If the need is not satisfied, it is subjectively experienced as discomfort, dissatisfaction, displeasure, frustrated feelings and wishes. JFM workers have to consider this factor as they are workers for socio-economic development of the society.

Knowledge of habit and skill of the participant is most essential for the J.F.M. workers in their working field. As externally, habits are similar to sills, they differ in their psychological nature. Skills are instruments that a person may or may not use. Habit, on the other hand, dominates man, and compels him to act in a given manner. Habit is as it were, an ingrown part of his personality. Participants are to be habituated to mutual understanding on various JFM occupational problems. JFM workers have to make continuous efforts to obtain high team efficiency of participants and perfomance. Astolyarenko rightly says – "persons who always agree with the boss are convenient but they are not always the best subordinates". This sentence is very important for JFM administrators. But immoral behaviour or irresponsibility cannot be forgiven. Talented persons mostly have certain individual traits for their duties. Administration of JFM organisation is of different nature as Lenin pointed out that work of administration requires people who know how to administer.

Criticism is one of the strong negative factors in J.F.M.

and it occures very off and on. When criticism occures it indicates –

1. Inadequate social training, 2. Low mentality level, 3. Emotional stress 4. Being frustrated due to dealing with circumstances beyond control, Criticism is a cutting edge and no one likes it.

Decision of J.F.M. workers (Forest Personnel) and participants is the basic foundation for the J.F.M. activities.

1. A decision is effective if it is realistic
2. A decision is effective if it is well times, well advised it will not have to be quickly rescinded or revised.
3. A decision is effective if it is substantial.
4. A decision is effective if it is sufficient.

Usually, many subordinates contribute to decision making. The best decisions are made by those who possess the best information. Three kinds of circumstances demand the decision of J.F.M. workers :

1. Instructions from higher echelons and he need to carry them through.
2. Information from lower echelons.
3. Independent detection of a problem which calls for a decision.

Any half hearted attempts will result in unconstructive activities. Hence, half hearted decision will never gives anything.

J.F.M. workers should not forget that years ago, before the age of steam, people travelled in sailing ships. The winds are often blowing from the wrong direction. Yet those old sea captains usually managed to keep their ships sailing towards ports and they were trying to reach the port. They did it by taking back and forth, and by setting the sails so that the wind would still carry them forward.

In J.F.M. sailing ship, the forest personnels are the captains and their port is the success of the J.F.M. movement.

J.F.M. is nothing but decentralization as the popular participation in Forest management. According to Lilienthal, the three essential characteristics of a decentralised administration are given as under :

(1) The greatest number of decisions should be made in the field, and with this end in view, the field officers must be so selected and trained as to develop the capacity to decide the questions on the spot.

(2) A decentralised management must develop, as far as possible, the active participation of the people themselves. Their co-operation and not mere compliance is essential.

(3) Co-ordination of the work of various agencies in the field should be made in the field itself because central co-ordination means delay, jealousies and jurisdictional disputes.

J.F.M. worker must be good supervisor, J.M. Pfiffner has listed eight qualities which a good supervisor has. These are –

(1) Command of job content means expert knowledge of the work to be supervised. But technical expertness by itself does not make a good supervisor.

(2) Personal qualifications are a co-operative spirit, evenness of temper and honesty, these qualities are more important to a supervisor than almost any other quality.

(3) Teaching ability requires no explanation.

(4) The general outlook of the supervision should be of faith and enthusiasm in worker with which he

is concerned, so that he may be able to lead those who work under him.

(5) Courage and fortitude imply that the supervisor should not be afraid of taking responsibility and decision.

(6) Ethical and moral considerations require the supervisor to be free from major vices generally condemned by society e.g., sex scandals and so forth.

(7) Administrative technology means capacity to organise co-ordinate and direct.

(8) Curiosity and intellctual ability means an attitude of mental alertness and flexibility and not being impervious to new ideas and practices.

Like others, in J.F.M. practice also, the classical theory of Luther Gullick and Lyndall Urwick is very important. They submitted a report viz. "Paper on the science of administration" to the Noble Peace Prize winner (In 1906), 26th President of U.S.A. Roosevelt on "spoils system" of civil administration of U.S.A., at that time, Gulick and Urwick declared seven scientific policies to reform the civil adminstration. The word POSDCORB whose each letter represents one policy, is given as under:

1. P. stands for Planning.
2. O. stands for Organising.
3. S. stands for Staffing.
4. D. stands for Directing.
5. Co. stands for Co-ordinating.
6. R. stands for Reporting.
7. B. stands for Budgeting.

Till this day the POSDCORB theory is not overruled by any theory in the field of management science. In J.F.M.

every body should remember the statement of F.W. Taylor that "Management is true science resting upon clearly fixed laws, rules and principles as foundation". J.F.M. of Assam is also having fixed laws, rules, and principles. The underlying principles of J.F.M. are the overall development of the forest dwellers besides the creation, and conservation of forests.

Lastly, in conclusion, we can say that "the rich get richer, the poor get children" should not be the principle of Joint Forest Management in Assam.

10

Prospect of Joint Forest Management at Dhubri District

Dhubri District of Assam is situated within 89.42° to 90.12° East Longitude and 26.22° to 25.28° North Latitude. The boundary of the district in North is Kokrajhar district, East is Goalpara district and Meghalaya (Garo Hills) South is West Bengal and Bangladesh. The total Geographical area of the district is 2,838 Sq. km. whose population is 13,32,475, out of which male population is 6,83,298 only (1991 census). The population density of this district is 470 per Sq. km. which is the highest among other districts of Assam. The average density of population in Assam is 286 only. From these figures of the density of population, one can easily imagine the problems of management, protection, extension and development of forests of this district. The over whelming population problem of this district is probably due to unprotected Indo-Bangla International Boundary and infiltration in this district. Population growth of the district head quarter, Dhubri town from 1901 to 1996 speaks the truth which is as follows :

Year	Total Population	Increased Population	Percentage
1901	3737	-	-
1911	5808	+2071	+55.42
1921	6707	+899	+15.54
1931	9435	+2728	+40.67
1941	12699	+3264	+34.59
1951	22787	+10088	+97.44
1961	28355	+5568	+24.43
1971	45589	+848	+28.74
1981	60000	+1441	+31.61
1991	76000	+1000	+11.10
1996	85705	+9705	+16.48

Considering this problem, the concept of Forest Management of Dhubri District is to be formulated with modern concept. All the past systems are now practically found almost out dated. During pre-independence period the main motto of forest conservation was to collect valuable trees and supply to different industries specially railway agencies for timber sleepers, leaving behind nothing to the neighbouring villages and forest dwellers. This fact is fully reflected in the Assam Forest Regulation, 1891 (Regulation 7 of 1891) where not a single word is found for the welfare of the surrounding people of forest. This idea is still prevailing more or less among the public of Dhubri district, even to some of the forest officials, not to speak of others. It is surprising that after the gap of half a century, the Assam Forest Regulation 1891 has not paid any attention towards the promotion of welfare of the people through the Article 38 of the Constitution of India. As a consequence, the condition of forests under Dhubri District it is deteriorating day by day, similar to the forest of other area. Presently, all the forests of Assam are hollowed by encroachment, illegal fellings, forest produce smuggling etc. from which forests of Dhubri District are also not free. Considering this, India emphasised on production of Forestry and Agriculture. This is the concept of involvement of local people in forest production, management etc. It was initiated in the name of Joint Forest Management (J.F.M.) system. In actual practice the J.F.M. is :

(1) A systematic arrangement to manage the forest with the co-operation of the local villagers.

(2) Forest department and the villagers protecting and developing the forest jointly.

(3) A partnership between the local people and forest department.

(4) Management of the forest resources, available near the village with the active participation of the

villagers and technical guidance from the forest department.

(5) Fulfilment of local needs taking into account the ecological balance.

(6) Management of forest by the villagers and the foresters jointly.

(7) Government and people protecting and managing forest jointly.

(8) To meet the local needs.

(9) A management agreement with the forest department.

(10) A bottom-up approach.

From this definition of J.F.M. is derived that it entails joint protection and mangement of forest by the forest department and the local communities whose object is to meet the local needs besides other demands.

In India, presently 20 states started J.F.M. system covering about 1.5 million hectares of forests where approximately 12000 forest protection committees (F.P.C.) are engaged. In Assam, Dhubri Forest Division is the pioneer in this matter and during 1997-1998 more than 60 of F.P.Cs. are formed having not less than 1000 members eagerly waiting for recognition. History of the formation of F.P.C. under Dhubri Forest Division was very interesting and the name of Sri K.N. Dev Goswami, I.F.S., the present chief conservator of Foresst, Social Forestry, Assam will be engraved on the pillar of stone. (In this case, attention is drawn to "people's involvement; key to protection of Dhubri Forest" by this writer and published in "The North East Times" Guwahati on 3rd Nov/98).

It is progressive sign that the system of Joint Forest Management in Assam is now accepted by the Government and the J.F.M. is the only means to protect the Forests of Dhubri District. A similar and provision was laid down at Social Forestry Project, Assam, where the provision for the participation of the local people would be attempted mainly through the community social forestry committee. The community social forestry committee is very similar to the Forest Protection Committtee under Joint Forest Management system. But this provision is not reflected in practice anywhere in Assam and as a result the man made forest remains as a Government property and the local people take it to be no body's property.

The F.P.C. committees under Dhubri District are having various scopes to develop the economical conditions of the local societies besides developing the forest by managing the forests scientifically; specially by rehabilitation of degraded forest from viable root stocks and gapfilling.This scheme is found very successful in Andhra Pradesh with the help of World Bank. Similar attempts were tried at Parura, Khudigaon forest under Dhubri District where from the viable root stocks of sal a good forest is now produced with the help of F.P. Committees. Out of the various problems in protection and preservation of forests, encroachment is the major problem. By carrying the load of encroachment, the way of development of forests is to be considered specially in Dhubri District. But special attention is to be paid to discourage the encroachers. As already stated, this District is thickly populated. Besides, more or less one third of the geographical area of the District consists of Chars, which are mostly unstable. Those chars are eroded during the flood seasons and the villagers are migrated to the nearby high lands or to the forests. This is the common practice each and every year and the civil authorities are facing lots of problems in rehabilitation of these villagers. This pressure obviously has to be faced by the forests of this district. To solve the problem, examples of neighbouring states like West Bengal and Tripura, the Joint Forest Management System can be tried specially in Dhubri District. In the notification of Joint Forest Management in Assam, it is proposed that the area under the protection of forest protection and Re-generation Committee may usually be limited to 3 Hect. per beneficiary for natural regeneration and 1 Hect. for intensive planting. The D.F.O. shall select the beneficiaries for consulting forests protection and regeneration committees in consultation with local panchayats. The committee is to ensure protection of forests and plantation etc. through the members of the committtee. This is the only system to preserve and expand the forests under Dhubri District. Local people are also found inclined presently towards the system of Joint Forest Management of this District. Only with this system, again the sal forest of Ex-Zamindary forest will smile with great joy. Simultaneously the local people will treat their surrounding forests as their own partnership property with forest department. As a result, the whole concept of forest management will be changed in the eyes of the local villagers of 1360 villages of Dhubri District.

Forestry and Agriculture are the ways to develop the rural people of Dhubri District. Hence, forestry and agriculture are to be equated by means of Agri-silvi, Farm forestry, J.F.M. etc. The industrial development of this district is very poor which is described here. Total small scale industries registered upto 31.12.90 at Assam 15908 numbers out of which only 323 number were at Dhubri District. (Statistical Hand Book : Assam 1992) Besides, there is no heavy industry situated in this District. Major livelihood of people of this district is only cultivation. The method of agriculture is also primitive as only 22779 Hect., area having irrigation facilities out of total 5,94,143 Hect. of area was irrigated in Assam during 1991-92. Hence considering all these factors we can easily came to the conclusion that J.F.M. is the only possible way to develop the condition of rural people of Dhubri by way of Agri-silvi system or introducing cash crops along with the Forest Plantations. In 1930, the then Silviculturist of Assam, C.J. Rowbotham I.F.S. recommended. Arhar dal (*cajanus Indicus*) to be raised as shelter crop within the plantation areas. [Assam Forest, Bulletins (No. 1 of 1930)]. This species is a good cash crop and can be raised in all plantations of Dhubri Forest Division. Sporadically, this is cultivated by the villagers for their own consumption but not as a commercial crop. In Dhubri district only 5000 Hect were found for Arhar dal cultivation during 1991-92. It is estimated that the country's population will be about 1350 million by 2020 A.D. and the country would then need a minimum of 30.3 million tonnes of pulses. It is now very painful to note that the per-capita availability of pulses has declined from 64g/capita/day (1951-56) to less than 40g/capita/day as against the FAO/WHO's recommendation of 80g/capita/day. But 55g/capita/day requirement of pulse is the realistic target if we take into account the total protein nutrition derived from milk and its products, eggs, fish, meat etc. The main characteristics of pulses including the Arhar dal are that they can be grown under harsh environmental conditions and their capacity to fix atmospheric nitrogen. During the process of evolution and adoption, pulses crops have acquired primitive characters like long duration, indeterminate growth, bushy habit, excessive flowering, flower drop, shattering, non-synchronous maturity, etc, for their survival rather than high yeild.

Arhar dal plant enriches the soil fertility and improves the soils structure as it fixes atmospheric nitrogen in their roots and thus improves soil fertility. The tap root system opens the soil into deeper strata and heavy leaf drop increases the soil organic matter. It is very ideal for mixed, intercropping system. This crop has an inherent quality to trap the soil moisture from deeper soil strata due to the tap root system. Arhar dal can be harvested upto three years from a single plant. So it is a very suitable inter cash crop within the plantations as no canopy is formed within three years of artificial plantations.

11

J.F.M. IS THE TOOL OF RURAL DEVELOPMENT

Joint Forest Management (J.F.M.) is an instrument for rural development specially for rural people of surrounding, or within forest areas. Rural development is a special concept, concerning, a multisectoral programme, involving development in productive agriculture including forest and its related services, individual activities, health, education, small savings etc. In one sentence, the development means the development of 'quality of life' of rural people 'Quality of life' is defined as a term widely used in bourgeois propaganda, sociology, philosophy and political economy in describing the conditions of life and work in present-day and future societies.

Exploiting the striving of working people in the capitalist countries to improve their social position and attain a qualitatively new standard of living, bourgeois ideologists are trying to reduce the struggle for a new "Q.L" to carry out reforms which do not go beyond the bounds of the capitalist system. They call for better public education, health services, protection of the environment and natural resources, and recognition of the dignity and value of the human personality. But the realization of these humanitarian aims is blocked by the selfish interests of the capitalist monopolies, which are concerned with increasing their profits and not with improving the well-being of working people.

In Marxist literature, there is a concept of a way of life which has a quantitative and a qualitative aspect. The former aspect is assessed by a system of indices of people's materials well-being and the later aspect, by the degree of social freedom they enjoy and the conditions the exists for the development of the personality, freedom from economic exploitation and from political, national, racial and all other oppression is provided by Socialism." (ABC Political Science: : Political Terms: A Short Guide). Indian democracy has a mixed economy with an avowed goal to establishing a "Socialist Pattern of Society". This underlying principle is reflected in Indian planning also, whose ultimate object is to improve the quality of life of the rural poor. Rural development is a multifacet framework involving a multi disciplinary approach. In this process, self help and community participation have a paramount role. Mr. Michael Walton, Director of World Bank's Poverty Reduction Programme said that one of the reasons of poverty in India is that rural poor are not participating in the economic growth. He stressed the need for ensuring increased participation of the poor and specially the rural poor in the economic growth, 'Non participation' is a fact, but it is also true that the poor villagers are not taught and are not welcome to participate in the developmental activities. Villagers are not asked to raise plantation, to construct a road or to dig a ringwell within their village. But these are going on through the method of target approach judgement of achievements which often are not only purtail but also false targets are fixed on a macro basis which does not ensure any specific localisation of activity in a particular village or are, also the target approach totally ignoring the qualitative aspects of a programme, means that assets once created are either ill maintained, destroyed, or become less effective.

There is the scope of decentralised planning which offers the best possible way for enlisting people's particpation in the process of planning and implementation of development programmes. After independence, the first rural development effort was the Community Development Programme in 1952. Unfortuntely, this C.D. movement completely isolated the forestry sector. However, "It was the first service-oriented programme whereas the administrative system of the country was firmly rooted in the basic law and order culture." (Perspective of Rural Development : Ramesh C. Misra) Presently, rural development is entrusted at the district level, District Rural Development Agency (Society)-DRDA, has been set up to adminster the programme. It is a society registered under the Registration of Societies Act, 1860, for undertaking rural development but as a Government agent, a forester can not deny the development of the rural people living inside the forest. For example, many tribal villages were included during the time of notification of reserve forests within Dhubri district. The development of those villagers can be denied by any forester (Forest Officers) of this division? Answer will be definitely "no". The villagers of Monglajhora, Bainaguri, etc. (All are within Monglajhora R.F.) which is the second largest R.F. of Dhubri Forest Division.

To develop the forests, forest dwellers must be developed and it is the responsibility and duty of a forester. Hence, it is essentially a people's programme which aims at securing active participation of the people for successful implementation. "However, in practice, the programme is carried out solely by official efforts. Participation of the people and their leaders is only symbolic to fulfill some formalities." (Rural Development strategy in the N.E. Region, B.P. Maithuni). Creating symbolic leaders with an object to satisfy formalities does not satisfy the idea of people's particpation. Villagers are basically flexible and resilient and adopt themselves well to their nature and sorroundings, specially at Assam. It is true, that rural poor, because of their long experience with unscrupulous landlords, moneylender, petty politicians, and bossing bureaucrats tend naturally to be suspicious and fearful, besides being superstitious and risk averse. For example, seventy five per cent of benefits in the form of timber were given to the Tribes of Dhubri from her forest. In long past, it was in coupe form and after the abolition of coupe, later it was in the lot timber form. But in reality, all the non-tribal timber contractors, droped the tender papers at tender box by taking simply the signatures of the tribal people. Many of such signatories were working as supervisor under those Non-Tribal timber contractors. Still many of Bakijai cases are pending against many tribals who once worked as Demi for Non-tribal contractors.

K. Singh, said - "Management of rural development means managing the process of rural development through planning, organising, staffing, directing, coordinating, monitoring, controlling evaluation of rural development programme." (Rural Development Management : India's Experience). As every body knows that where there is a management, there is manager. Managers may be a industrial manager or may be a rural development manager. Difference between the two is that if former one is treated as an olympic player then the later one will be the college tournament player. A manager need not be an expert in all the skills which he is directing. However, he should have an idea about the work acquired either by reading or through experience. A manager can successfully use the technical skill of others and he need not possess all the skills himself. Managers should know what type of skill is necessary for particular job so that they can enlist the help of that skill or the department engaged in the skill. Also manager should know the inter-relationship between the skills. This is important when a member of departments is involved in a work. What a minister does in his state, a captain does on the play-ground, the manager has to do in his organisation.

Do's and Don'ts came to be accumulated and the later generations of managers had no difficulty in adopting them. Management at this stage took to systematised practice of the past. However, this frequently resulted in a rigid and conservative attitude since many managers who had found these practices successful, refused to abandon them later when they had become out of date due to change of conditions. The managers of Assam Forest better, knew that the past system of management is out dated, but they (not all) refused to abandon the past system directly or indirectly they became hindering agents of people's participation in forestry management of Assam. Also, The Assam Joint (People's Participation) Forestry Management Rules, 1998 is an officially sponsored management rule imposed from the top, this rule was not designed to evoke people's initiative. For example, Rule II (i) attracts the provisions of Indian Forest Act, 1927, and Assam Forest Regulation, 1891; these Acts and Regulation found total failure at Assam to protect the forests. Also, the funds are not given to the Froest Protection and Regeneration committee though the functions are given to them (Rule 9), purely on 'bureaucratic nature'. So, the target groups become the recipients rather than active participants. However, the administrators, the politicians, the social-workers, the forester (Means in this book, as 'Forest officer' defined at Assam Forest Regulation, 1891) forest dwellers, should not be allowed to kill before the people's participation at Assam forest are truely born. No body try to extend hands for miscarriage of J.F.M. at Assam but it is every bodies duty to nourish the embrayos of J.F.M. and to get a healthy baby of participatory forest management.

J.F.M. was not born at heaven. The zygote of it was formed at Indian Soil (Bengal). X-cromosome was the social change and Y-cromosome was the protection of forests of this zygote. Social change is a process by which alteration occurs in the structure and functioning of a social system. Adoption or rejection is the common occurrence in this social system. Development is a type of social change in which new ideas are introduced into a social system in order to produce higher per capita incomes and levels of livings through more modern methods and (often) improved social organisation. The present era is certainly of direct contact change, caused by outsiders who, on their own or as representatives of programme of planned change, seek to introduced new ideas in order to achieve definite goals. For all this, communication plays the vital role; communication is the process by which messages are transferred from a source to a receiver, and is thus a vital concept explaining human behaviour thoughts etc. Simplified model communication process is S-M-C-R-E, a source (S) sends a message (M) via certain channels (C) to the receiving individual (R) who responds or reacts (Receiver) to this stimulus with an effect (E). M (message) must be technically correct, socially acceptable to the receiver, other wise C (Channels) will not respond properly. 'M' is there to plant a young seedling by the V.V.I.P himself at the place of his visit while addressing the public and the programme is still continuing at Assam. But in reality, it is found that 'C' had/have not responded at all, the season of planning of the planted areas was/is not considered. This planting is technically in correct and socially un-acceptable. As a result those innocent young seedlings are murdered. Similar case is in *van-mahotsava* also within Assam, as the season is not suitable for tree planting at this time. Response of receiver (R) depends upon the level of awareness, level of education, the social structure, the local aspiration etc. From, the above analysis, inference may be drawn that in the rural development of Assam 'S' and 'M' are diseased factors. These diseases have to be cured in J.F.M. programme to develop the rural people within the jurisdiction of Assam Forests. Any communication system concerning rural development merely with fulfilling targets of financial expenditure and physical macro targets has not delivered the programme in a true sense. It depends on the amount which brought about better income level or levels of living for the beneficiaries.

The DRDA which implements various anti-poverty programmes, it is still headed by the District Magistrate depsite a decision taken by the Central Government that it will be chaired by the Zila parishad's elected chief. In all states except Karnataka and West Bengal, the DRDA is dominated by the officialdom. In Assam DRDA is headed by the Deputy Commissioner as chairman and has a Project Director as a full time executive officer to assist the chairman. Project Director is assisted by several Assistant Project Officers each from different lines, except forest. Why a Forester's service as A.P.O. is not found necessary is not known. But the necessity of Forester as A.P.O. is felt at Andhra Pradesh. Without going more, an akin structure of DRDA is essential to implement J.M.P. at Assam, where D.F.O. will be the P.D., A.C.F. will function as A.P.O. Range officer's duty will be equivalent to B.D.O., Forester's duty shall be of the Extension officer and Forest Guard will serve as 'bare-foot doctor' for J.F.M. guidance to the villagers.

Bare-foot doctor to Project Director of Assam Forest is best known that the poverty of forest dwellers is the for different problems of Assam Forest. The writer, having an experiecne after serving one fourth of a century in executive cadre and as a field officer, it is experienced that the family having minimum five bighas (7.5 Bigha makes one hectare) of land, no members of these famalies are going to forest. Hence, it is very easy to provide the income of five Bighas of land through the J.F.M. programme of Assam, by which the action of saw and axe upon forest will be inactive.

Assam is one of the sisters of seven states of North-Eastern region of India. The region having 7.7 per cent of area which bears 4.40 per cent of population of the country. This region is connected with the rest of the country through a narrow corridor in North Bengal with a width of approximately 30 km. 2.55 Lakh Sq. km. (whole N.E. region) is linking through only 30 km. hence automatically the structure of society, economy, politics etc. is different in various respects with the rest of country. For instance, 21.75 per cent of the total population (5.78 million scheduled tribes) is scheduled tribes of this region, against 7.53 per cent of the country as a whole. There are 209 tribes in N.E. region out of which 23 in Assam. (Arunachal Pradesh-101, Manipur-28, Nagaland-20, Meghalaya-14, Tripura-18 and in Mizoram-5). Livestock population in this region is much more in comparison to its human population. It is seen that 36 cattle are found per 100 people, in North-Eastern Region, where 29 cattle per 100 people is the Indian average. But the production of milk is very low. Stall feeding is quite unknown to the villagers, which they are accustomed with free grazing system. This is the major problem of Assam Forest, specially in raising the new plantation at nearby villages. Diversity of culture, custom habit, tradition etc. (Not problem) leads to the non-acceptance of different development programmes by the villagers. As a result, the fruits of all development programmed is now "Interestingly, (one field officer), he also observed that when base line survey is done each year, the families are always reported to be lying below the poverty line." (Social Development strategy in the North East Region : B.P. Maithani). But what is poverty line and what is poverty? As we know, poverty is the income level which would enable a family to have a per capita daily consumption of 2400 calories in urban areas. In rural development programme, poor famalies are identified into three annual income groups :

1) Upto Rs. 1500
2) Rs. 1501 to Rs. 2500 and
3) Rs. 2501 to Rs. 3500

and preferencial group whose income is below 1500 which is called as 'Poorest of Poor'.

As J.F.M. is the instrument of rural development not only within or around forest but its hands can be extended to any areas which are not within the orbit of Assam Forest, such as huge riverine areas, silted agricultural fields, water logged areas which are neither fit for psciculture nor agriculture. Bhae (Salix) species is found very suitable in water logged areas of Assam, who grow naturally at Gaijan (Tinsukia). Peoples participation through J.F.M. is not very difficult at Assam, if the income of the participants can enhance up to Rs. 3500 per year. This can be achieved through cash-crop, dairy farming (Stall feeding), cultivation non timber forest produce, rasing timber producing fruits trees (Am, Kathal etc), within the selected areas of J.F.M.

K. Singh focussed– "In India, Government is the single most important agent of rural development and it attempts to plan, administer and implement rural development programmes through its departments and agencies. It is now, by and large, agreed that the existing Government Organisational Structure is not appropriate for rural development". (Rural Development Management : India's Experience). This truth may be reflected even at J.F.M. of Assam. A monkey and a fish were faced in a sudden flood. The monkey scrambled up a tree to safety, and the fish struggling against the current. Noticing this, the monkey was filled with humanitarian desire and rescued the fish from water current. Fish did not feel anything but the monkey was surprised that the fish was so ungrateful to him for the help. This fable illustrate clearly the relationship of 'change agent' and his rural people clients. Fish lives in water, and monkey lives on trees. Rural people (Not all) live under the line of poverty while 'change agents' are above this line. Change agents are the bureaucrates. "Bureaucracy has to be representable and responsive to social change, providing a organisational flexibility and adoption of administrative policies." (Rural Development: Management Strategy – S.K. Sharma). In the path of J.F.M., as a rural development, this fact is totally applicable. Forest Personnel of J.F.M., field of Assam must be a man commanding the confidence of the villages (within their jurisdiction) by virtue of his sharing of the same life style as in the village. Fortunately, Assam Forest team having this quality and this team spirit can cope with any national Forest team of India.

A good plan alone can not bring the desire results unless followed by careful implementation. No doubt, the Assam Joint People's participation, Forestry Management Rules, 1998 is a good plan. It requires careful implementation to get the desired results. With a clear policy enunciation, full political support, and needed administrative infrastructure, it is expected that the goals of rural development through J.F.M. will be achieved at Assam. Rural development is not a structured discipline Jon R. Moris points out that rural development is an area where the economist, the sociologist, the anthropologist, the political scientist, the psychologist, the scientists of various lines and the engineer will probably have almost equal stake in focussing their microscopes; and the approvals will be startlingly different. The subject of rural development covers the entire range of human problems. So to be a good rural developer through J.F.M., human problems have to be identified and tried to be solved with the available resources. Gunnar Myrdal, warned, "In the absence of more discipline – which will not appear without regulations backed by compulsion – all measures for rural upliftment will be largely ineffective". Hence,

J.F.M. regulation or Rules of Assam requires to be backed by compulsion at least for some days to get effective results.

There has been considerable criticism that the community development has been making the people more dependent on Government. This defective gene is to be eliminated, at the embryonic stage of J.F.M. practice at Assam. Participants are to be taught self dependence. The objectives and processes of J.F.M. are needed for bringing about permanent changes in the attitude of the people. Applied to planning of programmes, it is required that not only do we plan the activities and take up the work but also follow-up action that is needed to obtain the permanent and ultimate results we intend to achieve. At present, J.F.M. Rules of Assam N.G.O. and V.A. (Voluntary Association) are netting, [(Rule 7 (iii)] as N.G.O. has several advantages over Government Agencies. "It can have greater flexibility in its working than Government organisation can have, can allow full freedom to its field agencies to adopt programmes to changing local situations, can have freedom to experiment, can be free from rigid or externally imposed targets and can modify its programme schedules according to local circumstances. This indicates some of the weaknesses which Government Agencies inherently suffer from." (Community Development in India :: B. Mukherji, I.C.S.). The N.G.O. and V.A. of the locality shall be utilised for motivating and organising village communities as laid down in J.F.M. Rules of Assam [The Assam Joint (People's participation) Forestry Management Rules, 1998]. The function of N.G.O. & V.A. is to act as liaisoning agent between the Participants and Forest Department (Government Agency), and bridge between the Government and public. All Voluntary orgnaisations must be non-partisan and free from politics. It is a fact that the voluntary service has always been strong in India and it is strongest in Assam. For instance, there is the establishment and maintenance of various schools and colleges (Venture) at villages and towns by public, without having any financial assistance from Government. These schools and colleges are playing a vital role in education of Assam.

Community Development through J.F.M. is more technical and more complex than the normal Community Development Programme. As economic growth is brought about by a judicious application of labour and capital to natural resources (forest), is the main tool of J.F.M. So, to manage the forest with active CD-Operation of rural people for their benefits without disturbing the environment is technically a very critical job. It is not like other development works, such as construction of road, building etc. "The term environment means whole sum of the surrounding external conditions within which an organism, a community or an object exists. All the components of environment are inter-related and mutually inter-dependent. Another division is known as 'human environment' which includes conditions and situations formed by man.' (Degradation and Development of Environment - Zahid Hussain) J.F.M. is to protect and developed the environment (Physical) and even it should not disturb the human environment; falling which the pillars of J.F.M. will collapse, specially at Assam and other North East States. N.E. is the richest bio-diversity centre of Indian sub-continent. It's having more than 223 families of angiospermic flora, (Dicots - 184 families and monocots - 39 families) 650 spps. of orchids, 450 Spps. of grasses, 68 Spps. of bamboos etc. and the flora of this region exhbits Indo-Malayan affinity. Hence, Botanist consider North-East 'as a cradel of Plant evolution'. The soil is rich in organic matters, iron contents, but very low boron, calcium and zine, the pH. of soil usually ranges from 4.5 to 5.5. The rainfall and humidity is high, though rainfall in this region was below the average during 1990, 1991 and 1992. Average temperature of N.E. is continuously on the rise and problem of scarcity of water is facing. So, to protect and develop the existing angiosperms, orchids, grasses and bamboos etc. is one of the major task of J.F.M., as other rural development agencies do not penetrate deeper to this problem. Development can not be acheived without conserving the environment. Environment is the store house or godown of natural resources. Forest is one of the most valued ingredients of it. So to protect environment, forest must be protected through people's participation with the aim and intention to all round development of participants. According to A.S. Chauhan, some damage to the environment (Forests) has already occurred by introducing some exotic species at N.E. region including Assam.

"There is no denying the fact that sufficient finance has been allocated to the region (N.E.) but the pace of development has not been achieved". (Population Pressure on Forest Resources in the North Eastern Region – M.C. Pandey). Similar fate is met to J.F.M. programme of Assam. Funds are allotted to raise plantations to the Forest Department, targets are completed, but without participation of people. This is nothing but an insult to the forest dwellers of Assam in the eyes of Assam Government notification No: FRW. 8/93/75 dated 10th Nov. 1998. It may be an insult or salute but the J.F.M. is the emerging point of both the physical and human environment in Assam. J.F.M. started and it took the first step and it must keep on going towards his goal. No body should think in negative ways about the J.F.M. of Assam.

"Nobody can really guarantee the future. The best we can do is to make use of the chance, calculate the risk involved, estimate our ability to deal with them, and then make our plans with confidence."– Henry Ford II. Some danger to the environment (Forest) has already occurred by introducing some exotic species at N.F. Region in Assam. "To ensure enhanced energy Supply, a number of fast growing exotic tree species have been introduced into geographical area which are basically not suited to them and without sufficient base line information on their impact, ignoring large number of indigenous fast growing trees which have advantage of being more in harmony with the local environment and also have all the desired attributes of an exotic species, as far as possible, these fast growing exotic tree species should not be encouragd against the indigenous ones".

12

A Critic of Eco-socio System of Gauripur/Dhubri

Eco-socio means Economics and Society. Hundreds of definations can be quoted by any student of economics but the defination printed in the Wordsworth Encyclopaedia, which reads as – "Economics is the study of how, in a given society, choices, are made in the allocation of resources to produce goods and services from consumption and mechanism and principles that govern this process", is found more appropriate. Economics came of age as a seperate area of study with the publication of Adam Smith's The Wealth of Nation (1776). Again the word 'Society' is very difficult to describe though every body understands the meaning or feels it. We can say, society is a web of social relationship. Out of this social relationship, some are very simple and some are very complex, some are permanent and some temporary. Society is not merely a collection of individual beings, as it is not a group but a process of relationship. Society is an organisation, a system or a pattern of relationship among human beings. It would not be mistaken to say that in the absence of differentiation, the very existence of society may be threatened.

Raja Pratap Ch. Baruah, the then zamindar shifted from Rangamati to this place in 1856, which is now called Gauripur. The name of the place prior to 1856 could not be traced out though it was tried in several ways. It will be good research work if somebody came forward. Gauripur came to the limelight just 30 years of

Yandabo Treaty (1826). After the inactment of abolishment of zamindary system of Assam, 1952, this area comes under the preview of regular civil administration like other parts of Assam. Previously it was permanent settled area, fixed in 1793.

According to available records, "Gauripur town is important on the north bank of the Brahmaputra, in Gola Alamganj Paragana, which contains the residence of the richest land holder of the district (The Goalpara district) and where a small fair is held in September or October every year. The population, according to the census of 1872, was 1805" (Statistical account of Assam'. W.W. Hunter, Vol II). Remarkably, the population in 1872 in Dhubri was only 477 and it was estimated that Rs. 30,000 were earned annually by the Raja (Zamindar) of Purbatjowar during the last 19th century, as taxes or ceses termed 'Gor Kati' (felling timber) and 'Thaljat' (stacking timber). The predominent commercial timbers were sal (Shorea robusta). During 1870, 207.19 sq. kms were sal forest within this track which contains about 2.5 million of sal trees with a yield of about 25000 trees annually. The earnings, the resource producing sources, diverted to Calcutta for the interest of their own. Here, only how the economy of Gauripur was deprived in forestry sector is cited. Similar deprivation was going on in other sides also.

As already mentioned, only 1850 persons were at Gauripur and who were they? Surely they are the relatives, friends and workers of Raja. They all migrated to Gauripur leaving behind their own original societies. They formed a new society at Gauripur with full support and co-operation from 'Raj Families'. Gauripur society was developed on patronise style and assimilated to pure Assamese Society of Gauripurian society which starts in 1960, as the writer Dr. Dhiren Das has mentioned in his work 'O Mor hay hastir kanyare'. In this precious work, it is found from the statement of Mr. Ratenswar Ray

(Mantu), a renowned Retd. police officer that the Assamese language was taught in the school since 1948 only. The spare head person to introduce Assamese language at school was Trailakya Choudhury, Mahadev Sarma and then Manager of Gauripur Estate Chandi Barman. Even Gauri Nath Shastri delivered lecture from the chair of the president of Banga Sahitya Sava, held at Gauripur in 1934 that "we (Gauripurians) were never Bengalee nor Assamese". Society of Gauripur (within town area) is a homogeneous mixture of Ganga and Brahmaputra valley. Social migration from the banks of Kaveri and Godavari were not found. Hence social structure of Gauripur is complex since its formation. Also, presently 'urban driff' phenomenon is continuing due to various eco-socio reasons.

As per 1991 census, population of Dhubri District was 1325653 having density of 467 persons per sq. kms. which stands first within other districts of Assam. Rural population of this district was only 1164012. Literate persons were 390394 within Dhubri district as per the census report of 1991. It is an established fact that the increase of population is due to illegal migration from Bangladesh (present) as Dhubri district is the gateway. 'The Muslims have become majority groups in Dhubri (70.46%), Barpeta (56.07%), Goalpara (50.18%) and Hailakandi (35.42%) (Insurgency in North East India by B. Phukan, Page 246). It is covetous to quote that "In 1992, fourteen years after its formation, ULFA, for the first time, released a document written by publicity secretary, Arnab Hazarika alias Anirudha Choudhury, that acknowledges the positive role played by Bengalee Hindus in Education and Bengalee Muslim in Agricultural development in Assam'. (The External Linkage in Insurgency in India's North-East by Subir Bhowmik). It is rightly observed by Rafiuddin Ahmed in his "The Bengalee Muslim 1871-1906" that the majority of Muslims lived in the marshy, low-lying tracts of eastern Bengal. The area covering roughly the present Bangladesh. As a community, the Muslims were overwhelming rural in character and they contributed only a fraction of the urban population. Muslims of eastern Bengal belonged predominently to the cultivating class, while land holding, professionals were dominated by the high caste Hindus. The picture of past East Bengal or present Bangladesh is just similar to our Dhubri District. Bangladesh represents a Malthusian nightmare with two little food or too many people on too little land. It is one of the world's most densely populated and imperished state having 128 million people. The country's population density of 939/ sq. kms. is the world's highest. In Bangladesh land has always been as fluid as the water that shapes it. The geography of delta changes like speeded version of continental drift.' (Paul Harrison, The Third World Revolution : Environment, Population and a Sustainable World : London/NewYork :Tauries & Co. Ltd. 1992, p. 230). Every year new lands are formed due to river erosion by eating into the existing lands. The same business of nature is happening here also Economic structure (agro based) of southern bank of the Brahmaputra under Dhubri district has now totally collapsed. As the river Brahamaputra started rising more damage was caused towards the southern bank due to heavy deforestation of Northern bank.

Increase of population against the natural growth leads to various problems, such as socio-eco, socio-political, religion, culture, customs, even socio-physico. Presently, more or less all these problems are being faced by the people of Dhubri District. Bodo-Rajbanshi-Muslim-Hindu all are having the smell of all those problems. The microscopic looking of Narottam Gaan reflects as "induced by poverty and environmental degradation, between 12 to 17 million landless poor people in Bangladesh, search for land and economic livelihood, they have been migrating to neighbouring states of India, viz.

Assam, West Bengal, Tripura, Orissa and far away urban centres like Delhi and Bombay creating a sub-nation, the size of Australia within India. Though Bangladesh continues to proclaim that it has no illegal migrants in India, Bangladesh communities have sprung up in New Delhi and Bombay under the shelter of flyovers and in Muslim dominated regions. The political parties in India resort to political vote banks. The Government of India put the Bangladeshi migrant figure as about 1,00,000 but the intelligent sources estimated it as 2,00,000. Providing political advantage to political parties during hastling these refugees receive patronage in terms of education, development and health facilities even at the cost of the local inhabitants. This contains the seeds of further local conflicts.' (Environmental Degration and Conflicts, P. 109)

Under the pressure of immigrants, the Agro based economy of Dhubri district has already crossed the carrying capacity. Socially, they neither feel Assamese nor Bengalees. They want to establish their own identity by forgetting the actual truth that the back bone of socio-economic structure of all the existing societies of this belt is totally paralised. Of course, the question of building eco-socio structure of zamindary period is out of question. To survive a society, the economic viability is the most vital element. By producing a few lakhs of bricks and tiles it cannot attract the sustainable economy to the society.. (Present industrial position of Dhubri district). Dhubri is one of the largest jute producing centre but not a single centimeter of finished jute articles are produced at Dhubri. Products of all marshy and low laying areas are pumped out leaving behind nothing to the producers. Similar is the case in forest also. Forest of Dhubri is giving nothing to the local people except deprivation from all forest producers.

But, at present the forests of Assam as well as Dhubri have come forward to give equal shares to the forest dwellers. Assam Government issued a Notification No. 8/93/95 dated 10th Nov. 1998 as The Assam Joint (People's Participation) Forestry Management Rules, 1998 by which a volcanic change in the Forest Management will occur, which gives maximum benefits to the local people. Rule 5 of this notification reads as – "The area under the protection of committees may usually be limited to 3 (three) hectares per beneficiary family for natural regeneration and 1 (one) hectare for intensive planning". 'Hence in Dhubri district 512.40 sq. kms (51240 hects) of the forest area can be easily managed with maximum of 51240 people. Then the problem of encroachment and illegal felling does not arise. Dhubri district having only 18.05% of forest requires at least 33% of total geographical areas (Dhubri having 2838 sq. kms of area) failing which the problems of loss of fertility in agriculture field, loss of moisture retaining capacity of the soil, disturbance of ground water level, loss of top-soils, increased cutting capacity of river water during rainy seasons, formation of sand duns on the river banks during winter etc. will occur which are now happening at the Dhubri district.

As rural population is already larger than the urban population, hence the rural economy and society is more stronger than urban society and economy. The same truth is also applicable throughout India. Also, one cannot think that the political boundary is the boundary of economy. Even political boundary does not affect in social harmony also. 'Dheki pump' brought from Bangladesh is acclamatised at Dhubri for increased agricultural products but still not a single agri-engineer of Assam can invert, discover or produce a mechanical tiller whose cost is bearable by a marginal farmer.

Eco-socio conflicts (not problems) of Dhubri/Gauripur are not similar with other districts of Assam. Not going further, the statement of Soneswar Kailta, IAS (Retd.) "will the Assamese survive" will be appropriate "Sarat Singha is koch, Hiteswar Saikia is an Ahom so, they might pretend that they were the sons of King Narayana and King Rudra Singh though their forefathers were never at the thrones of Russia where Kalitas ruled for some years" (Page II), Now the situation has changed. What will Rudra Singha, King Narayana will give or the thrones of Russia will give anything to the Kalitas, similar is the case in Bodo also.

After discussing all this, one can conclude that the quotation of George Santayana "Society itself is an accident to the spirit, and if society in any of its form is to be justified morally, it must be justified at the bar of individual conscience."

Gauripurian (Dhubrian) society is moving a change of social and economic formation, a stage in society's progressive development based on a definite mode of production of material, which represents a unity of the productive forces and production relations. The following S.E.F. (Social and Economic Foundation) succeeded one another : primitive-communal system, slave-owning system, feudalism, capitalism and communism. Each S.E.F. has its own political and ideological superstructure (Ideas, Organizations and Institutions.)

13

Report of the Expert Group on People's Participation in Forest Management

An Expert Group (EG) was set up under aegis of National Afforestation and Eco-Development Board (NAEB) in 1993, to examine the issues related to people's participation in Forest Management. The complete text of the report is given below:

People's Participation in Forestry

The need to involve people in development activities is being increasingly recognised by the Government. The purpose is to make them own the process and product, and to empower them to manage it for their common good. Community Management, which is the ultimate manifestation of people's participation, is best suited to handle common property resources like forests. In India, however, for many historical reasons, the main being the colonial legacy, the legal ownership and management rights of forests remained vested in the state to the exclusion of the local communities. The fact that the state was not succeeding in its role became evident in recent decades : first there were not enough goods coming from the forests to fulfil community needs : second, the satellite imagery revealed the stark reality of forests degrading at a very rapid pace.

Joint Forest Management

The National Forest Policy, 1998 (NFP), made a significant departure while overhauling the National

Forest Policy of 1952. It recognised the need to involve the people in the development, protection and management of forests. The NFP declares. "The life of tribal communities and other poor living within and near forests revolves around forests. The rights and concessions enjoyed by them should be fully protecred forest including their domestic requirements of fuelwood-fodder-minor produce." Thus creating a massive people's movement with the involvement of women became the central concept of forest management policy. It is in this context that the Ministry of Environment and Forests issued the guidelines dated 1 June, 1990 concerning the involvement of village communities and voluntary agencies in the protection, development and management of forests, going by the expression of Joint Forest Management (JFM).

The Expert Group

The guidelines, endorsed to the State Governments, gave a formal framework of action. If envisaged an institutional arrangement for the local people to jointly (with the Government) protect and manage the forest resources in return for a share in the yields from it. The guidelines contained both path-showing and prescriptive provisions to enable the State to issue their own operational regulations. Over a period of three years, the operation of the guidelines through individual state Resolutions has thrown up several conflicts and issues. In this background, at the instance of National Afforestation and Eco-Development Board, an Expert Group (EG) was set up in July 1993 to examine the issues related to people's participation in forest management.

Current Status

At the time of the issuance of the guidelines, West Bengal and Orissa Government were already carrying out JFM activities with regulations, developed on their own.

The Central Government guidelines were instrumental, however, in making many other State Government issue appropriate notifications for launching JFM initiative. As of now, 14 States have issued resolutions/notifications besides West Bengal and Orissa. The list now includes Andhra Pradesh, Bihar, Gujarat, Haryana, Himachal Pradesh, Jammu and Kashmir, Karnataka, Madhya Pradesh, Maharashtra, Orissa, Punjab, Rajasthan, Tamil Nadu, Tripura, Uttar Pradesh and West Bengal.

There is no concrete information as regards the extent of forests managed under these regulations. Piecing together the estimates of various official and non-official agencies, it can be concluded that an extend of more than 1.5 m. ha or 15,000 Forest Protection Committee (FPCSs) compared to the total extent of degraded forest area in the country, which is 30.98 mha out of total forest area of 76.52 mha as per the state of the Forest Report of 1995, the coverage is modest. Considering the vastness of the spread of forests, different layers of state bureaucracy, people and NGOs involved, all of whom are yet to be fully sensitised to the concept, the progress is satisfactory. It just seems to be the right time to take a review to find out the issues being thrown up.

In terms of impact of the JFM concept of forest protection and management and no less important on the psyche of the important actors (the bureaucracy, people and the NGOs), studies and researches are few. However, available studies reveal a very positive picture. In Harda forest division of Hoshangabad district of Madhya Pradesh, after the JFM regime was introduced, it has been reported that the fuelwood production had increased four times. In Rajheria village of the same division, fodder production went up and yielded annual surplus of Rs. 20,000. In South-West Bengal, the net annual income of tribal households from non-timber forest produce (NTFP) has increased at Rs. 2523 per household and the

NTFP constituted 22 per cent of the household income. In Jammu region of Jammu and Kashmir, 5000 ha of both degraded forest and common lands were covered. There were reports of innovative efforts to invite people's participation from Surat Forest Division in Gujarat, Udaipur division in Rajasthan, Kundapur division in Karnataka and from the tribal-predominant forest tracts of Andhra Pradesh. The information availabe, in bits and pieces, is encouraging. Similarly the Aravali Afforestation Project in Haryana has been able to regenerate and plant up some 17000 ha of village common lands,without fencing by involving the people closely in the project activities. There is sufficient evidence from Orissa, Bihar, Andhra Pradesh, Gujarat and Karnataka to show that several village level communities have, in response to the deterioration in the conditions of their forests, taken up the task of protecting and regenerating them. They have done so through their own traditional institutions and their own self-abnegation. A lot can be learnt by a proper study of the dynamics of the self-initiated goups' approach towards protection and management of the forest areas.

Issues

The Expert Group collated several issues, brought out by various reports received on request from NAEB or otherwise from NGOs, individuals and other institutions who have shown interest in the subject in addition to the issues raised by the members. A sample of these issues is given below:

- The guidelines now very restrictive in their application to degraded forests only, should be extended to all kinds of forests, regardless of the quality of the forests and even to plantation raised before. Degraded forests also needed a precise definition.
- Women's role was ignored or kept marginal at decision making level in some State Resolutions.

- Rules varied in different States regarding, enrolment of members; some confined the membership to weaker sections; some to two members (husband and wife) in a family; widowed house-holds escaped attention altogether.
- The reference to "net income" as the basis for sharing in some State Resolutions created fears among FPCs that expenses could be exaggerated.
- There were complaints of micro-plans prepared by FPCs being found not acceptable to forest department for reasons of incompatibility with the existing working plans.
- In some places, a concept of village development fund was introduced; the fund was to be raised from a portion of the income of FPC and to be used specifically for village development. Some felt that the first charge on the fund should be of forest development.
- Blanket ban on grazing in JFM areas (prescribed in the guidelines), is not considered practicable in a village situation with lot of cattles around and therefore needed a change.
- There should be a forum, in place of binding jurisdiction of the forest department alone, to settle issues involving conflict between the department and FPC or other interests.
- Recognition and registration should be accorded to self-initiated FPCs with retrospective effect from the date they started functioning so that they can derive the benefits under the JFM regime, particularly those linked with the minimum period of functioning of FPC.

- JFM activities in some states having no donor-funded projects seemed to be constrained by lack of funds.
- Relation of FPC and Panchayat Raj institutions and possible conflicts needed and assessment.
- Issue of forests degradation in North-Eastern States where forest lands are owned by communities themselves or autonomous district councils should be addressed separately as JFM mechanism obviously did not apply.
- Exclusion of sancturies and national parks (protected area network) from JFM purview needed review.
- Introduction of appropriate courses on JFM in the curriculum of training institutions of forest department should be considered.
- Conflicts due to exercise of recorded rights of villagers, not being the members of FPC and sometimes as neighbours have to be solved.
- Need for market research and other research support for JFM activities.

Recommendations

Issues of Jurisdiction

Role of the Centre and the States : The EG felt that guidelines of Central Government could hardly address all the ramifications that keep arising specific issues of local relevance (eg. conflict in the exercise of recorded rights vis-a-vis FPC rights). Therefore, the issues in which the Centre should play a role should be isolated, leaving operational issues to the local levels/State Governments.

Setting up representative forums for conflict resolution : For a new concept like JFM, the learning process is continuous and therefore the Centre and States should set up separate institutions to deal with emerging situations and issues which fall in their purview. States may set up forums at State and district levels (if necessary at more local levels) clearly demarcating the nature of issues to be dealt at each level. The model followed by Andhra Pradesh in this regard may be considered. All interested parties like the FPCs, NGOs, Forest Department should figure in such forums.

Silvicultural and Ecological Issues

Working plan and microplan: The NFP 1988 has shifted the emphasis from the policy of managing forests for maximising commercial timber output and revenue to a new priority of producing subsistence requirments of the tribal and poor living in and around forests. The contents of the microplans of FPC, reflecting this emphasis, often come into conflict with traditional Working Plans in force. Sometimes ecological issues are raised on the Silvicultural system adopted. Taking into consideration once a micro-plan is approved by the competent authority, taking due care that is in conformity with National Forest Policy, it should be deemed to have superseded the working Plan of that area to that extent.

Extending JFM beyond degraded forests : Questions have been raised on the logic of restricting JFM concept to degraded forests and on excluding protected area network (PAN). It has been explained that eco-development programmes involving local people are implemented in PAN and that given the primary consideration or promoting wildlife, the emphasis is on other harmonious eco-development programmes, which are run on generic JFM philosophy. The expert group recommends that in such areas JFM approach should be further extended and strengthened. As regards extending JFM regime beyond degraded forests in non-protected areas, it is felt that extension to any such formation of new FPCs, regardless of degradation criteria or any other character of the forests, should be determined by the success of JFM in that region of the State. The details of arrangements for benefit sharing, etc. for non degraded areas may be formulated with due care.

Social and Cultural Issues

Criteria for membership and conduct of the meetings : It is seen that membership criterion for FPC varied from State to State. It is felt that restricting membership to any class would introduce divisiveness in the society which is counter productive to the object of bringing them together for a JFM regime. On equity considerations, it is felt that all adults of the village (regardless of gender) should be eligible to become members leaving the choice to the individual adults.

Mandatory role for women : It is noticed that the criteria for women to figure in decision making forums of the FPC varied widely. It is, therefore, recommended that 33 per cent of the membership of the Executive Management Committee be reserved for women. In addition, it may be laid down that 33 per cent of the participants in the meeting of this committee must be women to complete the quorum.

Restrictions on grazing : Livestock grazing is too important a social issue to be ignored while making a blanket provision to ban grazing from JFM areas. It is expected that the micro-plan addresses the issue of generating fodder reources.

Recognising self-initiated groups practising JFM : The EG has noted that there existed even before the JFM philosophy formally got introduced as a self initiated community management of forests, sometimes as on offshoot of ethnic (tribal) tradition or a result of self motivation of the local communities. There is sufficient evidence from Orissa, Bihar, Andhra, Gujarat and Karnataka of such instances. These groups seem to have essential elements of community concern for conservation of forests. It is strongly recommended that such institutions or groups performing the essential functions of a FPC be recognised and registered, after an inquiry or on the basis of record. The period of their existence may be given suitable weightage for them to derive benefits under the formal JFM regime.

Economic Issues

Gross income to be the reference point for computations : Many FPCs feel that it is difficult to ensure transparency in reckoning the departmental expenses and further more for FPC to have a say in such matters. Thus, the 'net income' as a starting point for computations of benefits could become a controversial issue. It is therefore, recommended that wherever monetary benefits are intended for the FPCs, the computations should be based on gross income and not on net income.

Village Forest Fund : Some State Resolutions refer to setting up a Village Development Fund using all or some income dervied by the FPCs. In the first place, it is very doubtful that all FPCs have large income generating forests to get funds of the order to tackle village level issues. Further, formal development institutions like Panchayat Raj formations already exist to attend to these needs. All these apart, the conservation and development needs of the forests must be fulfilled first to ensure sustainability of the source of income. Therefore, the fund depositary created shall be called Village Forest Development Fund. It is recommended that not less than 25 per cent of the share of the village community be deposited with the Village Forest Development Fund.

Other Issues

Investment in JFM : Views have been expressed that enough funds are not available in the States where donor-finance assisted forest projects do not exist. It has been pointed out that for managing 20 per cent of the country's geographical area of the forests, the Paln funds made available from the First Five Year Plan to the Sixth Five Year Plan have varied from 0.395 to 0.71 of the total Plan outlays. Only in the Seventh Five Year Plan, forestry got 1 per cent which fell, however to 0.9 per cent in the Eighth plan. The EG records its concern in this respect as lack of funds could lead to disenchantment among the FPCs and the JFM tempo may decelerate. Therefore, to accelerate the expansion of JFM, there is a need of a Centrally Sponsored Scheme of JFM.

There is a need to integrated JFM approach with watershed approach without diluting the concept and character of Forest Protection Committees formed under JFM arrangements.

Monitoring JFM activities : Though more than five years have passed since the JFM circular was issued by the Central Government, there has been no mechanism to document the progress of JFM in terms of member of FPCs functioning areas being covered and other related details that could give insights to assess the progress and general state of affairs. The EG recommends to set up an appropriate monitoring mechanism. Commitment to JFM activities should form part of the job description and performance evaluation of the forest officials.

Introduction of suitable curricula in professional institutions : JFM philosophy should become an integral part of the curricula of the forestry training designed for various categories of forestry professionals.

Issue of revised guidelines : It is considered that June 1, 1990 circular of the Government of India marked a new era in the philosphy of Forest Management. Therefore, it may be left as it is cancelling or amending it instead of issuing a revised circular. Revised guidelines may be issued based on the recommendations contained in this report.

Panchayats, JFM and Forest Protection Committees : A question was raised about the role of the Panchayat Raj institutions, they would have in the execution of JFM and their interface with FPCs. Some felt that the existing provisions for the panchayat representation in the FPCs are adequate. Yet, some others pointed out that the elected representation in the FPCs are adequate. Yet, some others pointed out that the elected representatives under statutory provisions mandated by the Constitution would need to be closely associated with natural resource management and cited the case of West Bengal. Another view was that decentralisation means participation of more people in the governance and, therefore, concentration of all functions in panchayats may deprive a number of people who are not elected political members of the Panchayats but have been elected to the Executive Committee of the FPCs. Yet another view was that political governance through panchayats and direct resource management by people should not be mixed up. It will be inappropriate to consider the participation of elected representatives as substitute for common people performing a management role. It was felt that the matter needed deeper consideration. This is an aspect that might be addressed when the legal backing is considered for the JFM resolutions issued by various States; as on now they have all informal arrangements with doubtful legal rights for enforcement through a judicial system.

The concept of Van Mukhiya militates against JFM philosophy. The Expert Group is of opinion that it would create more problems to the concept of participatory management. It feels that the withdrawal of Van Mukhiya institutions and related orders should be seriously considered.

Problems of forests in North-eastern region : Some concern was expressed about the increasing degradation of forests in the North-east as registered in successive report of 'State of Forest' periodically brought out by Forest Survey of India. One particular reason, according to a view, was that substantial extents of forests belonged to their Autonomous District Councils or the communities themselves where the JFM dispensation perse did not seem to percolate and fit in. Moreover, interactive mechanisms with such district councils and the communities owning forests did not seem to exist. This matter needs further examination by an Expert Group, which may be constituted.

National level working group on JFM : The Expert Group recommends that a standing committee, somewhat corresponding to the one recommended at the State level, should be set up at the national level. Such an institution could comprise members of different skills, specialities and interests bearing on JFM Philosophy, (2) have an advisory role on matters referring to it and (3) evaluate the progress from time to time in different states. A national level conference on JFM should be held every year in which the policy makers, officials and the grass-root level organisations working at the field level should participate.

14

The Forests of Assam

Lying approximately betwen 89.4 E and 96 E logitudes and 24.10 N to 28 latitudes, the State of Assam is made up of two large valleys – Brahmaputra and Barak valley with intervening Central Assam Hills Range forming the watershed between the two valleys. To the north of the state lie the Bhutan hills and the hills of Arunachal Pradesh which are part of the Eastern Himalyan Range, the Eastern Border being limited by Arunachal, Nagaland and Manipur and the Mizo hills from the southern flank; on the west lies Bangladesh and in the extreme south lies East Tripura. The majestic Brahmaputra, to which the valley owes its existence and wealth of Agricultural resources, flows roughly from east to west covering a meandering course of about 750 kms before taking a southernly course and passing on to Bangladesh. Since the two main rivers flow in roughly east-west directions, the major tributaries are oriented roughly north-south directions.

The variations in altitudes in Assam ranges between 50 metres to about 1,00 metres, the highest point being met within the Barali Range of the North Cacher hills. The climate is typical subtropical monsoon climate; the range of average annual rainfall varies from 1,000 mm to 7,000 mm in different locations, minimum cold season temperature varies near freezing to about 15C; maximum temperature ranges 20 to over 41C.

It can be claimed that no other part of the world, with comparable climate, geotropical and conditions, there are diversities of the flora and fauna, as are found in the North-Eastern Region of India, of which Assam is a constituent State. The area is a meeting ground for the Indian, Tibetan and Burmese flora and fauna, and besides migration, considerable number of species must have evolved in the region itself. As many as 51 different forest types and subtypes have been recognised for the region as per latest all India classification, but even then the variations into the classifications are felt not to be adequately covered. The forests of Assam are located in (i) an interrupted strip of varying along the foothills of the northern boundary (ii) scattered hills and hillocks in the two valleys (iii) part of the area of the Central Assam Hills range and (iv) alluvial terraces and undulations in the plains. The brief data on the forests of Assam is furnished below:

1. Total Geographical Area — 78,523 Sq. kms
2. Gross area under reserved forests :
   - State — 17,051 Sq. kms
   - District Council — 1,749 Sq. kms
   - 18,8000 Sq. kms
3. % of reserved forest to total geographical area — 23.8%
4. ----Do---- Plains — 21.8%
5. ----Do---- Hills — 31.7%
6. Approximate areas under different forest type :
   - a) Tropical evergreen — 2,235 Sq. kms
   - b) Semi-evergreen — 220 Sq. kms
   - c) Moist mixed deciduous — 13,965 Sq. kms
   - d) Other including bamboo brakes — 2,380 Sq. kms
7. Area of reserved forests per capita brakes (Census 1971) — .0012 Sq. kms

8. Revenue and expenditure (Approximately in lakhs rounded off figures)

Year	Expenditure			Revenue	Net surplus or
	Plan	Non-plan	Total		deficit
1976-77	167	173	340	791	(+) 451
1977-78	237	570	807	966	(+) 159
1978-79	385	379	752	1135	(+) 422
1879-80	735	520	1255	1250	(-) 5

9. Approximate annual returns :
(average annual of 1979-80 and 1980-81)

a) Industrial Wood = 196 lakhs, M3
value Rs. 516 lakhs

b) Fuel Wood = 85 thousand, M3
value Rs. 14 lakhs

c) Minor Forest produce ---- -----
value Rs. 37 lakhs

10. Forest based industries:

Plywood mills	41 Nos.
Match Factory	265 Nos.
Matchsplint Factory	1 Nos.
Paper Mills	1 Nos.
Katha Factory	2 Nos.
Ivory Carving Industry	6 Nos.
Timber treatment and seasoning plant	3 Nos.

(There are other small cottage scale units also dealing in cabinet making, cane works, bamboo works)

11. Area dedicated to wildlife - 6.3% of gross reserved

Areas dedicated to wildlife	Forest Area Approx Area
Kaziranga National Park	430 sq. kms
Manas Sanctuary	390 sq. kms
Orang	72 sq. kms
Pabha	49 sq. kms

Pabitora	16 sq. kms
Sonai Rupai	156 sq. kms.
Garampani Sanctuary	6 sq. kms.

12. Distinctive rare fauna in Assam :

One horned Asian rhino, only Indianape_Hoolock Gibbon, Golden Langur, Clouded leopard, Black Panther, Golden Cat, Slow Lorris, Pigmy Hog, Hispid Hare, Binturong (Beer Cat), White Winged Wood Duck, Florican.

13. Tiger Project

One of the 11 tiger projects in India. In Assam, with Manas Wildlife Sanctuary as core area. From 41 tiger counted in core area in 1976, the latest census in 1980 shows the presence of 78 tigers in core area.

14. Estimated present figures of animal population of the state (for some animals only)

Rhino	1,200 Nos.
Tiger	300 Nos.
Elephant	4000-5000 Nos.
Buffalo	2,100 Nos.

15. Current regeneration efforts :

Plywood	1,785 Hects.
Teak	1,150 Hects.
Match wood	924 Hects.
Fuel wood	1,400 Hects.
Others	8,1444 Hects.

16. Social forestry efforts (1980-81)

Outside reserve forest and recreation forestry and community	538 Hects.
Forests	262 Hects.

17. Organisation set up :

a)	No. of circles	: Territorial	5 Nos.
		: Functional	4 Nos.
b)	No. of divisions	: Territorial	24 Nos.
		: Functional	20 Nos.
c)	No. of range		112 Nos.

18. No. of gazetted staff — 115 Nos.

No. of non-gazetted staff — 5068 Nos.

(By Courtesy of Assam Forest Department)

15

Assam Forest at a Glance

1. The State :			
Area	..... 1971		78523 Sq. Km.
Latitude	.....	.....	20° (N) 28° (N)
Longitude	.....	.....	90° (E) 96° (E)
Rainfall	.....	.....	1000 mm to 2500 mm.
Temperature	.....	.....	Min. 50°C Max 38°C
Average annual Humidity	.....	.....	80%
Total Population	..... 1971		146 Lakh
Estimated Population	..... 1981		199 Lakh (As on 31st March)
2. Forest Area			
Reserved Forest	.... 1982-83		17272.98 Sq.km.
Proposed R.F.	..... do	.....	3370.78 Sq.km.
Unclassed State Forest	..... do	.....	10063.81 Sq.km.
Total Forest Area	..... do	.....	30707.57 Sq.km.
3. No. of Reserved Forest	..... do	.....	304 Nos.

4. (a) P.C. of Forest area to geographical area 39%

   (b) P.C. of R.F. area to geographical area 22%

   (c) P.C. of R.F. area to total Forest area 56%

   (d) Per Capita Forest 1971 Popln. ..... 0.0021 Sq.km.

5. Forest Villages (1982-83)

No.	Area	Population
524	52903 ha	1,50,233 Nos.

6. Encroachment (1982-83)

Area	No. of encroachers
1.31.197 hectares	70,264 households

7. Revenue & Expenditure (Rs in Lakhs)

Year		Total Revenue		Total Expenditure
1979-80	.....	1135.29	.....	677.23
1980-81	.....	1227.81	.....	1111.04
1981-82	.....	1524.53	.....	1233.45
1982-83	.....	1791.01	.....	1516.32
1983-84	.....	2202.21	.....	1870.45

8. Revenue from Different Forest Products 1982-83 (Rs. in lakhs)

(a) Timber	.....	.....	1484.37
(b) Fuelwood	.....	.....	30.77
(c) Bamboos	.....	.....	8.85
(d) Stone, Gravel, Sand	.....	.....	115.56
(e) Other Produce	.....	.....	81.79
(f) Miscellaneous	.....	.....	89.67

9. Outturn of Forest Products (1980-81)

Timber (logs)	.....	.....	341841 Cum
Timber (Poles)	.....	.....	383259 Rm
Fuelwood	.....	.....	212222 St. Cum
Bamboo	.....	.....	1117 ('000 Nos.)
Stone	.....	.....	1083 ('000 Cum)
Sand	.....	.....	690 ('000 Cum)
Thatch	.....	.....	14191 ('000 bdls)
Cane	.....	.....	25 ('000 bdls)

10. Supply of Some Major Forest Products

(i) Sleepers	1982-83	10,669 (Cum)
(ii) Matchwood	1982-83	10,000 (Cum)
(iii) Plywood	1982-83	58,700 (Cum)

11. Regeneration & Plantation (Area in Hectares)

	during 83-84	Upto 83-84
A. Production Forestry		
i) Fast growing species	2290	25691
ii) Regeneration	2035	32191
iii) Rehabilitation of degraded Forest	310	12356
vi) Matchwood	815	15254
vii) Minor Forest Produce Medicinal Plantation	10	243
Total Area	8469	121198
B. Social Forestry		
i) Social Forestry	5500	10289

	ii) Social Forestry including rural fuel wood	4600	7800
12.	20-Point Programme (1983-84)		
	a) Seedlings planted under Afforestation Programme		361.9 lakh
	b) Seedlings distributed to public		62.0 lakh
13.	Road & Communication		
	Total length of Forest Roads (as on 31.03.84)		3988 Km.
	(a) Gravelled		983 Km.
	(b) Fair weather road		3005 Km.
14.	Forest Based Industries (1983)		
	Plywood Mills		40 Nos.
	Saw Mills		365 Nos.
	Match Factory		1 No.
	Match Splint Factory		2 Nos.
	Paper Mills		1 No.
	Paper Mills		(Under construction)
	Hard Board Factory		1 No.
	Ivory Industries		6 Nos.
	Timber Treatment & Seasoning		3 Nos.
15.	Wild Life		
	(a) Area under National Park & Sanctuaries	1983-84	1182 Sq. km.
	Kaziranga National Park	1983-84	430 Sq km.

Wild Life Sanctuaries and Game Reserves (1983-84)

Kachugaon Game Reserve	139 Sq. km.
Manas Sanctuary	390 Sq. km.
Orang Game Reserve	72 Sq. km.
Pobha Game Reserve	49 Sq. km.
Laokhowa Wild Life Sanctuary	70 Sq. km.
Garampani Wild Life Sanctuary	6 Sq. km.
Barnadi Wild Life Sanctuary	26 Sq. km.

Field Project Under Project Tiger

Area under Tiger Reserve :

Core-Monas Wild Life Sanctuary	390 Sq. km.
Buffer-Sonkosh to Dhonsiri	2447 Sq. km.

(B) Animal Population (Nos)

		Kaziranga (1978 Census)	State (Estimated)
1.	Rhinoceros	939	1300
2.	Elephant	780	over 4000
3.	Buffalo	660	-----
4.	Bison	25	-----
5.	Tiger	40	-----
6.	Leopard	10	-----
7.	Sloth Deer	30	-----
8.	Sambar	300	-----
9.	Swamp Deer	700	-----
10.	Hong Deer	8000-9000	-----
11.	Barking Deer	130	-----
12.	Wild Pig	800-900	-----

(C) State Zoo cum Botanical Garden

(i)	Area	1983-84		1.30 Sq Km.
(ii)	Animals	do	Species (No)	Total Population (No)
	Mammals	do	62	354
	Birds		58	476
	Reptiles		7	39

(iii) Revenue Collected 1983-84 Rs. 4,31,307.70

(iv) No. of Visitors 1983-84 4,41,795 (Nos)

16. Organisation (83-84)

		Circles	Divisions
(a)	Total No.	8	45
	Territorial	5	22
	Functional	3	23
(b)	No. of Ranges	83-84	144 Nos.
(c)	Staff Position	31.3.84	6006 Nos.
	Gazetted	do	456 Nos.
	Non Gazetted	do	5550 Nos.

LIST OF RESERVED FOREST

District : Goalpara

Division : Goalpara

1. Phaphanga.
2. Gendabari
3. Uppertola Jhar
4. Sagen Bahi
5. Geradubi
6. Zangrazangsa Hills
7. Bardal
8. Dipkai
9. Dwaraka
10. Saikiabhasa
11. Bandarmatha
12. Nalbari
13. Kanyakushi
14. Athiabari
15. Kathakuthi
16. Bagmara
17. Deosila
18. Ambuk
19. Chitalmari
20. Kechabal
21. Chakuari
22. Budlung
23. Ghagra Hills
24. Rendu
25. Matia
26. Kalibari
27. Dewlee
28. Katimara
29. Borjhar
30. Rokhapara
31. Pancharatna
32. Dashikata
33. Lankui
34. Dakuakata
35. Ajgar Hills
36. Chatabari
37. Dabil Hills
38. Khoyopara
39. Nalanga
40. Depalchang
41. Bamundenga
42. Kumarkhail
43. Dhanubhanga
44. Nakkati
45. Ganbino
46. Dhamar
47. Salpara
48. Allibari
49. Moghajhar
50. Rangapathar
51. Paikan

District : Dhubri

Division : Dhubri

52. Rupshi
53. Lalkura
54. Monglajhora

55. Bamunjhara
56. Atharakutha
57. Silkjikhata
58. Didumari
59. Mahamaya
60. Bhelakupa
61. Paraura
62. Chandardinga
63. Sakati
64. Tilapara
65. Katrigasa
66. Chakrasila Hills
67. Sarpamari
68. Dudhnath Hills
69. Srigram
70. Tiptai
71. Guma

District : Kokrajhar

Division : Haltagaon

72. Ripu
73. Kachugaon

Division : Haltagaon

74. Chirang
75. Sathbendi
76. Nandangiri
77. Bhaskamar
78. Arearjhar

Division : Aie Valley

79. Bergtal
80. Sissobari
81. Teklai
82. Katribari
83. Kakaijana Hills
84. Bamungaon
85. Rakhalthakur Hills
86. Nakati
87. Monas (Part)
88. Digdari.

District: Barpeta

Division : North Kamrup

89. Deodhara
90. Betabari
91. Kuklung
92. Monas (Part)

District : Kamrup

Division : Kamrup East

100. Chaygaon
101. Dhuniagaon
102. Ghorapota
103. Kawasing
104. Jarasal
105. Rani
106. Maliata Hills
107. Garbhanga
108. Hajo
109. Silda
110. Aigathuri
111. Khanapara
112. Silapathar
113. Amchang
114. Gondhmow

115. Fatasil
116. Gopeswari
117. Aprikhala
118. Digheswari

Division : Kamrup West

119. Borjuli
120. Joipur
121. Nampahar
122. Baradebha
123. Gizang
124. Mugkhal
125. Sursuria
126. Kurkhari
127. Garubaladah
128. Teraibari
129. Khatkhati Hills
130. Khakrisikrbura Hills
131. Dumpara
132. Simla Hills
133. Dudkuri
134. Luki
135. Singra
136. Moman
137. Dimali
138. Khatajuli
139. Melaghat
140. Gohaingurung
141. Jharikhuri
142. Milmilia
143. Kulsi plantation
144. Patan
145. Barduar
146. Mayang Hills
147. Mataikhar

Division : North Kamrup

148. Subankhata
149. Marapagladia
150. Darranga
151. Kurua Hills
152. Baman
153. Khaligduar
154. Bornadi

District : Darrang & Sonitpur

Division : Darrang West

155. Kochmara
156. Balipara
157. Singrimara
158. Charduar
159. Singri Hills
160. Bhomoragri
161. Rowta
162. Burachapari
163. Bhirabkuna

District : Sonitpur

Division : Darrang West

164. Gahpur
165. Biswanath
166. Behali
167. Panpur
168. Naduar

District : Nagaon

Division : Nagaon

169. Kaki (Part)
170. Lumding
171. Dijer Valley
172. Suang
173. Bamuni
174. Kukrakata
175. Bagser
176. Deosur
177. Borpani
178. Lutumar
179. Khelahat
180. Borbari
181. Killing
182. Raja Mayang
183. Dhuadalani
184. Tetelia Baghara
185. Sonaikusi
186. Daboka
187. Jamuna Madanga
188. Kapahitali
189. Hahai
190. Hawaipur
191. Komorakata
192. Kamakhya Hills
193. Pilkhana
194. Pabitara
195. 1st addn. to Jokata
196. Lowkhowa

District : Jorhat

Division : Golahat

197. Doyang
198. Upper Daigrung
199. Lower Daigrung
200. Nambor (Part)
201. Rengma
202. Diphu

Division : Sibsagar

203. Geleki
204. Tiru Hills
205. Desai
206. Desai Valley
207. Hollongapar

Division : E.A. Wild Life

208. Kaziranga
209. Panbari

District : Sibasagar

Division : Sibasagar

210. Panidihing
211. Diroi
212. Abhaypur
213. Solah
214. Sapekhati
215. Dilli

District : Lakhimpur

Division : Lakhimpur

216. Ranga
217. Dulung
218. Kakai
219. Kaddam
220. Pabha
221. Subansiri
222. Simen
223. Archia Dimow
224. Jidhal
225. Zamzing
226. Sengajan
227. Gali
228. Paba
229. Sissi

(By Courtesy of Assam Forest Department)

16

THE ASSAM JOINT (PEOPLE'S PARTICIPATION) FORESTRY MANAGEMENT RULES, 1998

1. Short Title and Commencement

(i) The Rules shall be called "Assam Joint (People's Participation) Forestry Management Rules, 1998.

(ii) They shall come into force with immediate effect.

2. Defination : In these respects unless there is anything repugnant in the subject or context

(a) "State" means the State of Assam;

(b) "Governor" means the Governor of Assam

(c) "Government" means the Government of Assam;

(d) "Committee" means the Forest Protection and Regeneration Committee

(e) "Usufruets" means – use and profit of the benefits accrued from the property but not the property.

(f) "Minor Forest Produce" includes leaves, twigs of trees, edible fungi, medicinal plants, fodder, fruits, reeds and moss, silk, cocoon, wax myrobalan, lac;

(g) "Beneficiary" means the members of the Forest Protection and Regeneration Committee the unit of which is a family;

(h) "Working scheme" means the short term scheme formulated for regeneration, protection and management of forest, jointly by the members of Forest Protection and Regeneration Committee and the Forest Department keeping in view the needs and aspirations of the Committee Members;

(i) "Natural regeneration" means Regeneration of a forest natural seedfall with or without human aids;

(j) "Intensive planting" Man made plantation with much larger number of seedlings than the number of matured number of trees sustainable under a given set of locality factors;

3. Committee : There shall be a Committee namely "Forest Protection and Regeneration Committee" to be constituted under provision of rule 7 for the purpose of regeneration, maintenance and protection of forest areas in the State acting as members of the Committee shall be allowed, as a measure of incentive, usufructs defined herein-before in rule.

Subject to observance of the conditions provided in these rules.

4. Selection of Area : The sites including all areas outside Reserve Forest and only peripheral degraded areas of Reserve Forest shall be selected in accordance with a working scheme prepared in consultation with the beneficiaries and duly approved by the concerned circle Conservator of Forests.

5. Limitation : The area under the protection of such Committees may usually be limited to 3 (three) hectares per beneficiary family for natural regeneration and 1 (one) hectare for intensive planning. The area for natural regeneration and artificial regeneration will depend upon number of beneficiary families in the Committee. The performance of the Committees shall be closely monitored and the extent or limit of the area reviewed and revised if considered necessary.

6. Cost : The cost of regeneration and maintenance of degraded forest and allied scheme, for development work as per the approved schemes shall be borne by the Government.

7. Constitution : (i) Each Range Officer shall organise meeting with villagers of one or cluster of villages residing adjacent to forest areas and explain the concepts of Joint Forestry Management and its benefits in simple language and the President or some members of the local Gaon Panchayat will be invited to attend. In case, a minimum of 50% of the total number of adults in the village accepts the proposal of Forest Protection and Regeneration Committee proposal in the meeting then the Divisional Forest Officer shall constitute the Forest Protection and Regeneration Committee(s) within the framework of these Rules. (ii) The option to become members of the Committee shall be open to all the concerned villagers, living in th vicinity of forest concerned. Membership of each family will be in the name of the husband and wife or a male and a female member to the family and shall be considered as one unit of beneficiary. The families who are already entitled to rights, concessions or privileges over the forest area shall also be included as member of the Committee. (iii) Committee of the Non-Government Organisation (N.G.O.) and Voluntary Associations (V.As.) of the locality shall be utilised for motivating and organising village communities living close to the forests selected for protection, regeneration and afforestation etc.

The Non-Government Organizations (N.G.Os) and voluntary Associations (V.As.) may be associated as interface between the Forest Department and Village Communities. No ownership or lease right over the forest land will be given to the beneficiaries or to the N.G.Os V.As. No act in contravention of the provisions of Forest (Conservation) Act, 1980 shall be permitted.

(iv) Each Forest Protection and Regeneration Committee shall have an Executive Committee to carry out various activities as assigned to the Forest Protection and Regeneration Committee.

(v) The composition of the Executive Committee shall be as follows :

(a) Gaonbra or any member of the local Goan Panchayat(s)..Member.

(b) Elected representative of the beneficiaries (not exceeding 9) ....Member.

(c) Concerned Beat Officer or any Forest Official not below the rank of Forester deputed for the purpose...............................Member-Secretary.

(vi) The member of the Executive Committee shall elect the President in each meeting.

(vii) Constitution of the Forest Protection and Regeneration Committee including Executive Committee will be approved by the Divisional Forest Officer concerned on the recommendation of the concerned Range Officer.

(viii) The concerned Divisional Forest Officer will monitor, supervise and review the functions of the Forest Protection and Regeneration Committee.

(ix) If any change in the Forest Protection and Regeneration Committee or the Executive Committee is necessitated, after initial constitution, the Executive Committee shall make suitable recommendation to the Divisional Forest Officer concerned duly endorsed by the concerned Range Officer for approval.

(x) The Beat Officer, or the Forest Officer as the case may be, as Member – Secretary, shall convene the meeting of the Executive Committee at least once in every three months and once in every 6 months for the Forest Protection and Regeneration Committee.

(xi) The representative of the beneficiaries for the Executive Committee shall be elected each year in the annual general meeting of the Committee, where the concerned Range Officer shall be an observer.

8. Meeting and Quorum

(i) Forest Protection and Regeneration Committee shall maintain a register showing necessary particulars of the members of the Committee, e.g. name, father's name, address, number of family members, name of the nominee etc. The nomination forms duly filled in and approved by the concerned Divisional Forest Officer should be pasted in the register. Such register shall also be maintained by the concerned Range Officer of the Forest Department for permanent record.

(ii) The Forest Protection and Regeneration Committee shall maintain a "Minutes Book" wherein proceedings of the meeting of the Executive Committee held from time to time as well as proceedings of the annual general meeting of the Forest Protection and Regeneration Committee shall be recorded under the signature of the Chairperson of the Executive Committee and such minutes duly attested shall be checked by the concerned Range Officer for record and initiating any action proposed in the resolutions adopted in the meeting.

(iii) The Forest Protection and Regeneration Committee (to be referred to as the Committee hereinafter) shall hold an annual general meeting once every year where activities of the Committee as well as details of distribution of usufructuary benefits shall be discussed, besides electing representative of the beneficiaries to the Executive Committee.

(iv) The quorum of the meetings of the above Committees shall be treated as complete if 1/3rd of the members are present in the meeting.

9. Duties and Functions : The duties and functions of the Forest Protection and Regeneration Committee shall be as follows:

(a) (i) To ensure protection of forests/plantation through the member of the Committee.

(ii) To protect the forests/plantation(s) with the members of the Committee : The forest area selected for joint forest management shall be worked out in accordance with approved working plan/working scheme for subsequent revision preparation of working plan/working scheme, the Executive Committees of the Forest Protection and Regeneration Committees shall be consulted for working plan prescriptions in the forest area taken up for joint forest management. It shall also be ensured that no grazing, of cattle and other animals is permitted in the forest land under joint forest management but permission for cutting and carrying of grass and fodder as permissible silviculturally shall be allowed free of cost to encourage stall feeding of cattle and other animals. Improved varieties of Non-wood Forest Produce shall also form a component in the plantation activities.

(iii) To report to the Forest officials any attempted tresspass or wilful damage to or theft in the forest(s)/plantation(s) by any person or persons.

(iv) To prevent any tresspass or encroachment on grazing, fire or theft in or damage to any forest/ plantation or use of such land for agricultural purposes.

(v) To apprehend or assist the Forest Officials in apprehending any such person or persons committing any of the offences mentioned above.

b (i) To ensure smooth and timely execution of all forestry works taken up in the area under protection by the Committee.

(ii) To involve every member of the Committee in the matter of protection of Forest(s)/Plantation(s) as well as other duties assigned to the Committee.

(iii) To assist the concerned Forest Officials in the matter of selection/engaging labourers required for forestry works mainly from the beneficiaries and their families.

c (i) To ensure smooth harvesting of the forest produce by the Forest Department.

(ii) To assist the concerned Forest Officials in proper distribution of the earmarked portion of the usufructs among the eligible members of the Committee.

(iii) To ensure that usufructuary rights allowed by the Government are not in any way misused by any member and the forest/plantation sites are kept free from any encroachment whatsoever.

d (i) To prevent any activities in contravention of the provisions of the Indian Forest Act, 1927 or the Assam Forest Regulation, 1891 or any other relevant Acts/Rules.

(ii) To report to the concerned Beat Officer/Range Officer about the activities of a beneficiary which are found prejudicial and detrimental to the interest of particular plantation of forest, which may result in cancellation of the membership of the erring beneficiary.

(iii) To assist the Forest Officials to take action or proceed under the Assam Forest Regulation, 1891, the Indian Forest Act, 1972, The Wildlife (Protection) Act, 1972 and any other Acts or Rules against the offender, including any erring member of the Committee found to be violating the Provision of such Acts, and Rules on damaging the Forests/Plantations.

e) To ensure protection of wildlife in such areas.

f) To ensure protection all forests/plantations in areas other than the areas taken up for, participatory management within the jurisdiction of the respective village/villages from which members of the aforesaid Committee have been drawn, by preventing any tresspass encroachment or grazing, fire or theft or damage to any forest/plantation, and by generation and by generally assisting the Forest Officials in their lawful function in prevention of such forest offences and prosecution of the offenders.

G) To ensure that none of the beneficiaries included under the participatory management.

10. Usufructuary Benefits

(i) In case of natural regeneration/plantations taken up under the scheme, the beneficiaries shall have to protect the forest to be eligible for sharing of usufructs under this programme.

(ii) The beneficiaries shall be permitted to collect minor forest produces free of cost without causing any damage to the forest/plantations.

(iii) 25 per cent output from silvicultural things shall be set aside for distribution to the beneficiary families through the Executive Committee for meeting their bonafide house hold needs. In case of short fall, the Executive Committee shall prioritise the examination of the requirements of the individuals and arrange smooth distribution. In case of surplus, the Forest Department will dispose it off through the approved system of sale and deposit the sale proceeds in the fund of the Forest Protection and Regeneration Committee for utilisation for the cause of common interest of the beneficiaries. Balance 75% shall be disposed of by the Forest Department and 1/3rd of the net receipt (after deduction of proportionate cost of creation and harvest) shall be deposited to the Executive Committee for proportionate distribution to the members of the Forest Protection and Regeneration Committee.

(iv) The output from the harvest from main fellings shall be sold by the Forest Department. The beneficiaries will be entitled to 25% of the net receipts from main fellings. The net receipt will mean the sale value of the produce less the direct cost of creation and harvest. The concerned Divisional Forest Officer shall set apart proportionate amount from the sale proceeds as above and shall arrange distribution of the same to the eligible beneficiaries in Consultation with the Executive Committee upon satisfactory performance of the duties and functions detailed here-in-before.

(v) The receipt from the harvest of plantation under Social Forestry shall be distributed as above, amongst the beneficiaries after deduction of cost of plantation and cost of harvest.

11. (i) Failure to comply with any of the conditions laid down hereinbefore or contravention of the provisions of the Indian Forest Act, 1927 or the Assam Forest Regulation, 1981 or other relevant Acts or Rules, may entail cancellation of individual membership and/or dissolution of the Executive Committee on Forest Protection and Regeneration Committee as the case may be, without paying compensation to any one for any work that might have been done prior to such cancellation, by the concerned Divisional Forest Officer.

(ii) The concerned Divisional Forest Officer, shall be competent to take appropriate action and even to dissolve any Executive Committee, on the grounds stated above, on the recomendation of the concerned Range Officer or otherwise.

(iii) The concerned Divisional Forest Officer, may authorise the concerned Range Officer to take proper action and even membership of an individual member on above mentioned grounds, on the recommendation of the Executive Committee of Forest Protection and Regeneration Committee.

(iv) Appeal against any such penal action by the Range Officer may be preferred to the concerned Divisional Forest Officer.

(v) Appeal against any such penal action by the Divisional Forest Officer may be preferred to the concerned Circle Conservator of forests, whose decision shall be final. The format for the memorandum of understanding to be adopted by the Forest Protection and Regeneration Committee formed by the village comunity is given below :

Memorandum of Understanding

We, the member of the .... Forest Protection and Regeneration Committee do hereby undertake to perform the duties and functions as detailed in the Rule No..........................dated......................of the Forest Department, Government of Assam for proper protection of the forests/plantation assigned to this Committee as per the Schedule given hereunder :

Schedule

1. Name of Forest Protection and Regeneration Committee
2. District
3. Sub-Division
4. Police Station
5. Mouza
6. Panchayat
7. Status of the land
8. Area in Hectares
9. Boundary

    North- East-

    South- West-

We understand that the usufructuary benefits as detailed in the aforesaid Rule dated.................shall be allowed only upon satisfactory performance of the duties and functions by this Committee and the individual beneficiaries as per the aforesaid Rule.

A copy of the aforesaid Rule is annexed herewith duly signed by us on every page as proof/evidence of our having understood the same in letter and spirit.

Signature of the members of the Committee		Signature of Witness	
Name and Address	Signature	Name and Address	Signature
1. ____________	________	____________	________
2. ____________	________	____________	________
3. ____________	________	____________	________
4. ____________	________	____________	________
5. ____________	________	____________	________
6. ____________	________	____________	________

SIGNATURE OF LOCAL FOREST OFFICIALS

Sl.No.	Name & Designation	Signature
1.	____________________	____________
2.	____________________	____________
3.	____________________	____________
4.	____________________	____________
5.	____________________	____________
6.	____________________	____________

INDEX

L

M